SILENT PIGEONS COO

Drawing of Anthony Lawton age 76 by Julian Gordon Mitchell.

Silent Pigeons Coo

The story of Anthony Lawton's fight against progressive sensory loss

'A unique and balanced story
of a deaf-blind man
passionate to succeed
in the mainstream'

Paul Simpson
Co-National Executive Officer BATOD

JOHN MOORE

Silent Pigeons Coo

First edition 2023

© John Moore 2023

A CIP catalogue record for this book is available from the British Library.

Contents

Acknowledgements

I could not have written this book without the help of so many people. My wife, Jan, for her repeated proof readings, corrections and literary insights and years of patience; Anthony's family and friends and colleagues from the former Thames Water hydrometrics department. My neighbour, Katie Baker, for ongoing encouragement, Sarah Lawton for checking against defamatory content, Daniel & Rachel Masters for researching the family tree. Kenneth Bannerman of the charity Airfields of Britain for his detailed knowledge of the RAF during War II, Curators of the Royal Berkshire Hospital Museum and Elaine & Eli Tal-El for their help with the work of Dr Daniel Ling OC. I am especially grateful to Paul Simpson, co-National Executive Officers for BATOD (British Association of Teachers of the Deaf) and Edward Moore, Trustee of the Ewing and Ovingdean Hall Foundations (whose introduction came through Anita Grover CEO of Auditory Verbal UK). Their valuable encouragement and generosity in reading and advising on sensitive chapters regarding deaf issues and education, insightful guidance on the use of inclusive language, overall knowledge of deaf issues and especially Paul's remarkable eye to detail, have resulted in a better narrative. Thanks are also due to the Jubilee Sailing Trust for photographs of The *Lord Nelson* tall ship, Nigel Poole a former trustee and Robin Ready for details from the log he kept of the voyage to Australia. I would also like to thank the trustees of the Royal Berkshire Hospital Museum, the artist Julian Gordon Mitchell for the inside cover sketch of the 76-year old Anthony and Lorraine Hillier for providing the Hot Gossip Coffee-house for a fringe presentation during the Henley Literary Festival 2021. I am particularly indebted to Andrew Evans of Andrew Evans Design for his knowledge of publishing and book design. Apologies to anyone I have forgotten to acknowledge for their help over the five years it has taken to research and write this mixed-genre memoir.

'The prevalence of Usher syndrome varies from country to country, but it is a rare condition affecting approximately 1 in 10,000 people . . . so far, researchers have found 11 genes that are associated with the three main subtypes of the syndrome. Usher syndrome occurs equally in both genders and is always inherited in a recessive pattern, meaning that both a person's copies of the gene must be faulty for the condition to occur.'

– Retina UK

'I often think that the night is more alive
and more richly coloured than the day'
Vincent Van Gogh

'The mind is its own place, and in itself
can make a heaven of hell, a hell of heaven'
John Milton, Paradise Lost

'When you pass through the waters, I will be with you;
And through the rivers, they shall not overflow you.
When you walk through the fire, you shall not be burned,
Nor shall the flame scorch you'

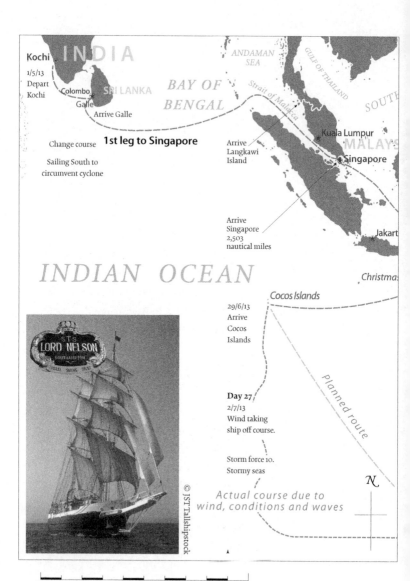

Kochi

1/5/13
Depart
Kochi

INDIA

Colombo
Galle
Arrive Galle

SRI LANKA

ANDAMAN
SEA

BAY OF
BENGAL

Strait of Malacca

GULF OF THAILAND

Change course   **1st leg to Singapore**

Sailing South to
circumvent cyclone

Arrive
Langkawi
Island

Kuala Lumpur

MALAYS

Singapore

SOUTH

Arrive
Singapore
2,503
nautical miles

Jakart

INDIAN OCEAN

Christmas

Cocos Islands

29/6/13
Arrive
Cocos
Islands

STS
LORD NELSON
SOUTHAMPTON

Day 27
2/7/13
Wind taking
ship off course.

Planned route

Storm force 10.
Stormy seas

N

© JST Tallshipstock

*Actual course due to
wind, conditions and waves*

1,000 miles

Map of the route take by the *Lord Nelson*.

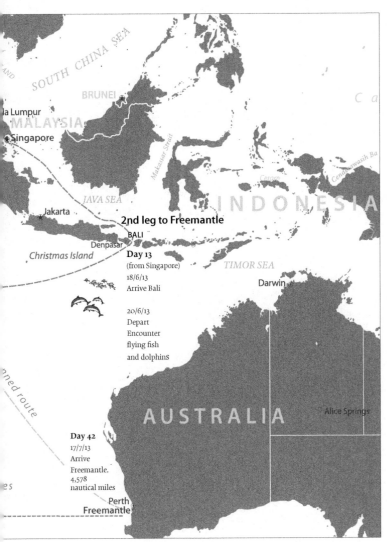

SOUTH CHINA SEA

BRUNEI

la Lumpur

MALAYSIA

Singapore

Makassar Strait

JAVA SEA

Jakarta

INDONESIA

2nd leg to Freemantle

BALI

Denpasar

Christmas Island

TIMOR SEA

Darwin

Day 13
(from Singapore)
18/6/13
Arrive Bali

20/6/13
Depart
Encounter
flying fish
and dolphins

nned route

AUSTRALIA

Alice Springs

Day 42
17/7/13
Arrive
Freemantle.
4,578
nautical miles

Perth
Freemantle

Map by Andrew Evans

This book is dedicated to my wife.
'The woman with her feet on the ground . . .
Revd. Graham Ingram 1936–2017

1

Silent Pigeons Coo

Anthony feels his way around the chessboard and a picture reforms in his mind. He makes an aggressive move. Checkmate. He reclines in his armchair and cherished moments float in his memory as he smells the fragrance of fresh cut grass at the tennis club. It is early afternoon in June 2019. Silent pigeons coo in nearby trees. Strangers occupy his childhood home in Fernbrook Road. His family have long since gone. Now all is still. He senses the presence of Chrissie and therefore she is there. He sees the Thames glistening in the sunlight as he replaces a mechanical water meter while balancing on a narrow concrete ridge. He sees the uniform of Squadron Leader John Shaw and admires his father with the eyes of a child.

He speaks and his mother corrects his pronunciation to the point of angry frustration. Out of sight but thronging around him the dinghy fleet competes for the finishing line. He holds his nerve and his position amongst the hearing and able sighted. Along a converted railway track he cycles at full speed feeling the movement of pebbles spitting beneath the tyres of his tandem. He is racing with friends. TV and press chase him for a story about his extreme charity-supporting adventures. 'My condition does not stop me and I refuse to be different. Some days I struggle . . .' he tells the journalist.

The sun is shining. He knows this because he can detect light and dark. Unseen and unheard the early summer breeze is rustling leaves in the trees around his house. He protests his unsuitability for jury service at Reading Crown Court and the Disability Liaison Officer explains why his dual *sensory loss makes him a perfect candidate. The Professor of Ophthalmol-ogy at the John Radcliffe Eye Hospital in Oxford examines the 73 year old man and asks 'do you have distant cousins who married somewhere in your family history?'*

It is a seminal moment.

Today is a good day for walking. The sun is not strong enough to trigger painful flashes in Anthony's retina or optic nerve. He is heading for the park which is rimmed by a main road. They reach the pedestrian crossing and Hesta stops. There is no traffic but it is part of her discipline to warn Anthony they are at the edge of the road. Anthony with two powerful hearing aids must use them to listen for approaching cars. He cannot hear traffic and commands Hesta to cross. She will only do so if it is safe. Their lives and wellbeing depend on her canine intelligence.

Anthony hears the presence of people electronically and looks at the invisible audience. He delays speaking and then asks; 'if tonight you had to sacrifice your hearing or vision which sense would you be willing to lose?' Discomfort momentarily fills the room as it has done so many times before. Most people choose to retain their ability to see but after listening to the deaf-blind septuagenarian many opt for hearing after he explains that this sense above all others keeps you connected to the bigger world. You can converse with life.

He is presenting on behalf of the Guide Dog Association and retells the moment he applied for his first guide dog. 'Do you want a girl or boy dog'? He is asked. 'A girl dog' he answers.

'Why a girl dog'? asks the assessor.

'Because girls are more sensible than boys'. The audience laughs and he apologises. Breaking minor conventions comes easily to him after the pretence of living a normal life. Disability motivated him to discover deeper resources within himself a long time ago. Later he would discover that self-sufficiency can be a double-edged sword. He would chase a dream as his father John had done before him. John wanted to become a wartime pilot. The speaker wanted to speak.

Anthony is standing at the bar of a social club and he hands me a beer. This is my first recollection of him. It is the mid-seventies and Abba fills the airwaves. I boast of planning a sailing trip across the Atlantic having barely sailed a dinghy on inland waters. By contrast he is a seasoned dinghy sailor. It was here that he met Rowena, a nuclear physicist. They married two years later but the relationship succumbed a decade later to the tensions that can arise between deaf and hearing partners. In 1977 a group of us rented a house close to the university. This included Anthony, two students and an academic in Food Science, Dr Mike Lewis, who would become a lifelong friend. In those days none of us realised the difficulties Anthony was privately experiencing. To all outward appearances his accomplishments seemed quite ordinary: a technical qualification in civil engineering and employment with a major utilities company. He was popular and also a skilled tennis player. Yet only he knew the lifelong struggle to achieve these modest accomplishments and the secret daily struggle to hold on to them. This life he led was the fulfilment of a childhood dream and it had a symbol: an MGB sports car. This was his statement of independence. Its function exceeded the car's ability to connect different parts of his life over tarmac. Yet behind his failing eyes and severe hearing loss lurked a man struggling to retain a grip on the prize he had sought to win throughout his childhood: the ability to communicate with mainstream society.

The challenges Anthony experienced during this time he kept to himself along with the knowledge that they were destined to become more testing with every passing year. Since early childhood he had been preparing himself for the uncertainty ahead by continually relearning. It helped him build an engineering career by lip reading and pretending to have clear hearing. This fortitude helped him escape crushing grief under sail whilst crossing the Indian Ocean when deaf and blind in his sixties. He started going blind from the age of sixteen. Anthony and I have something in common. He was born with a 70 decibel hearing loss classified as moderate-to-severe. There are different causes of hearing loss: conductive, sensorineural and mixed. From early records it seems Anthony suffered mixed hearing loss although his hearing problems were not recognised until well after his birth. Today he cannot hear anything without technological help.

I was born with good ears but an inability to listen at the appropriate time. This made learning difficult and teachers angry. Beginning life in inner city Birmingham also bequeathed a weak respiratory system and bronchitis from the factory chimneys of Tyseley. Deafness or bronchitis stuck to us like unwelcome friends throughout our early childhoods holding us back. Bronchitis deflected the trajectory of my infant education to an open air school from the age of eight. The educational standards were not high but moving from an inner-city industrial area to the Warwickshire countryside was transformative. Decades later I read about rumours of pupils being buried beneath the orchard between 1947 and 1950[1] but there are no surviving records from the era. The school has long since been replaced by a residential development. Perhaps the ornate building was too expensive to maintain for the benefit of unpromising, underprivileged children?

Anthony went straight to a school for the 'deaf and dumb' in Berkshire aged four and a half. His experience was transformative for different reasons. I appreciated the escape to the countryside but for Anthony a repressive pedagogy forged deep resentment and frustration. In his early teens he would attend the similarly labelled Deaf & Dumb Social Club in Reading where enforced expectations would drive him away from the silent-visual world forever. Early school for Anthony was a place of isolation, alienation and great loneliness. 'Learning' he says 'was minimal'. There are many contributing factors to learning difficulties. Anthony's were caused by a congenital hearing disorder but even with good ears he would have always struggled with language-based subjects and maths and science would prove to be his métier. He was gifted a bright mind and healthy physique but in 1950 there were no alternatives for bright boys with malfunctioning ears. He was barred from mainstream education until the age of nine. The effort to compensate for a 70 decibel hearing loss would provide Anthony with a deeply disciplined adult mind capable of visualising a chess board five moves in advance and the resilience to undertake dangerous escapades such as wing walking for charity in his seventies. This fortitude makes life in his seventies fulfilling but it came at a price which he began to pay from the age of four. Whatever fortitude was required in 1950 he would find it within himself. It was the widow's mite; it cost him everything with every moment focussed on surviving the current ordeal. He looks towards the audience,

'I joined an archery club. How do you handle a bow and arrow if you can't see?' He asks and jokes that the membership is going down. The remark is guaranteed a collective chuckle. 'But most importantly I love talking to people because it makes me part of life. Those of you who are born with all your faculties might think those born with less are disadvantaged but my deaf teacher, Dr Daniel Ling, once said, 'You learn from suffering as much as from joy'.

This is Anthony's story but it is as much about Anthony's mother and father. When their lives entwined the young couple would have had little notion of the challenge of raising a child born deaf and diagnosed at sixteen with the genetic condition retinitis pigmentosa, predicting he would be blind by his fortieth birthday. DNA analysis would later identify Usher type 2 Syndrome. The parents would reach a juncture where biological and psychological issues buried deep within their family histories would surface to introduce new and unwelcome directions that will impact Anthony and his brothers.

Anthony swims in time. The past is always with him. It both haunts and encourages. It gives him buoyancy and restricts his movements and like water is potentially dangerous as he would discover when struggling to survive bereavement in later life. But even at the lowest moment hope returned to nurture his future. His story does not exist in isolation. People's lives collide with other lives helping or impeding wellbeing.

Today, Anthony is walking his guide dog Hesta. She is the third female to change his life. She freed him from the exhaustive discipline of using a red and white cane. The colours denote he is a deaf-blind person. There was a time he felt shame and a perceived stigma of being disabled. It was mostly in his mind as people willingly stepped aside and smiled kind thoughts. Those days of pride and of hiding his limited faculties have long since passed. He is much more sensible now. He instructs people who are going blind of the necessity to use a cane and although its use is not obligatory Anthony would argue it is advisory. There are other less forgiving teachers of the blind such as concrete steps, brick walls and metal lamp posts. Instead of an advisory vibration through the cane as it strikes an obstacle they deliver sharp admonishing blows and Anthony, who at 76 is a little frailer than in his heyday, does not want to receive any more cuts and bruises or risk a leg-wrestling pothole. It is now 2021 and Anthony is being reviewed for a replacement guide dog. Hesta is tired. He has to demonstrate his proficiency when walking with a cane. It is a condition of dog ownership. Its correct use displays caution, common sense and a careful owner. There is a shortage of Guide Dogs and he may not receive a replacement. This is deeply worrying to someone who lives alone. Hesta is a true companion; a sacred life who combines companionship with guardianship. Guide dogs have a working life of ten years. It is a demanding occupation.

The two of them have full diaries although Hesta cannot be with him all the time. She cannot accompany him to Reading Football Club where his dual sensory loss allows him a front row seat. In 2020 the world changed. People are afraid of Coronavirus. Restrictions apply. The bus is a no-no. He hopes by 2021 they can escape their semi-incarcerated lives. He has received a double jab. Even so he needs to take precautions as it is far from clear the virus has been defeated. Alas 2021 is a difficult year. Life is opening up and closing down as Covid reinvents itself threatening Anthony's fragile connection to the outside world. And today they need to exercise. This means going out into the world he cannot see and can barely hear. Further difficulties are caused by an infection that has perforated an ear drum resulting in an 80 decibel average hearing loss – clinically defined as severe. Once again his ability to perform normal routines is complicated. Every day presents continuous challenges that hearing-seeing people are spared. He fights frustration. Never swears. If he makes a mistake he will start again. There is no alternative for a deaf blind man living alone. He refuses to capitulate. He must always seek and value hope. His right ear is distorting sounds and so he removes the hearing aid thinking it will make life slightly easier. It doesn't. With only one functioning ear he does not know where sounds are coming from. If a car approaches it is just the sound of an approaching car. If he is taken to a social event he struggles with the fluctuating crescendo of sound rising and falling around him. If someone speaks he cannot detect whether the person is on his left or right or in front of him and he is as likely to turn away as face them. Even though he is invited to the event and people know about his condition he is embarrassed – the emotional baggage of decades of rigorous self-reliance. The experiment to live with one ear limited to 80 decibel hearing loss has to end. He thinks a cochlear implant would be better but the consultant at the Royal Berkshire Hospital tells him it is better to rely on the last vestige of natural sound before receiving an implant. Even now at seventy six he pushes against any sense of limitation. The year 2022 promises exhilarating freedoms but wherever Anthony goes it will be within a dark semi-silent bubble – illuminated by an inner resource. He is sailing around the Ionian Islands and an active member of a crew of five. He needs to respond to commands: ease the jib, tighten the main, jibe, tack or adjust course. He feels the wind on his face and changes in the movement of the boat and he knows adjustments need to be made but he also needs to hear the instruction so that his corrections are synchronised with those of the crew. They are not deaf or blind but he expects equal treatment. When they head for the taverna in the evening he is exhausted and struggles to participate in the bonhomie but he doesn't mind. He is not there for the ride.

An operation to repair the hole in the right ear drum is urgently needed but now he knows it is irreparable. He is afraid of becoming isolated. His only channel of communication with the outside world might be through his sense of touch but he has never relied solely on cutaneous sensations before. It is just another challenge and challenges, like waves, have been crashing on Anthony's beach since 1946.

2

Isle of Man

The Isle of Man is a dramatic place where for much of the time strong winds drive rain clouds across remote ridges, the central valley and flat northern plain. Anthony does not remember the mild wet winter that followed his birth and the formal gardens or wild glens that nurture palm trees. Although the peaks are small they have an imposing stature due to their close proximity to the sea and define the landscape as they stride across the island dividing valley from plain. They exist only in his subconscious baby mind exerting their influence. It is a fitting birthplace for someone who would become as rugged as gorse.

In the 1930s the island had been identified as a suitable area for military airfields and RAF Jurby and RAF Andreas were completed in 1940 just in time to counter the extended bombing range of the Luftwaffe following the fall of France. One of the Luftwaffe's key targets was the neighbouring Port of Liverpool. The city had only recently played a central role in the Shaw and Lawton family history. John Shaw survived the war to tell of his own adventures in the skies over England and overland in West Africa. His personal contribution to the war effort was mentioned in a dispatch for distinguished service published in the Public Notices section of the London Gazette on 1st January

1945 which recorded 'His Majesty's high appreciation.' The Squadron Leader and his family were posted to the Isle of Man at the end of the war but John knew that as an RAF Regular he could be summoned at any time to support short-or long-term projects within the crumbling British Empire or with coalition partners such as NATO.

Anthony Eldred Shaw was born on a grey November morning in 1946 in Douglas. The evergreen gorse and heather that gives pink, lilac, purple and yellow tints to the hills and moorlands have by this time of year ceased to flower. His parents Gwendoline Shaw (nee Lawton) and future Squadron Leader John Shaw had married in North Wales in July 1941. Lichen-coated tombstones on the Little Orme, Llandudno witness the ceremony with featureless disinterest as large rollers coming off the Irish Sea smash themselves against Welsh cliffs. The name Eldred was given in remembrance of a Norfolk boy who could have become a deeply loved uncle but died at a young age. Anthony was the second of three boys. He arrived on time and was a healthy baby according to a speech written by his mother and presented to the Royal Berkshire Hospital in 1972.

John had wanted to train as an RAF fighter-pilot but the career he craved as a youth never materialised. This probably saved his life. He served briefly in Singapore before returning to Britain for pilot training just weeks before the unexpected fall of the British colony. After failing the pilot test due to poor eyesight he was offered a commission in the communications branch of the RAF known as Signals. His future seemed assured until he was summoned to join the war against Japan. The annihilation of Hiroshima and Nagasaki intervened and rendered this service unnecessary. The family remained on the island but with the Cold War now approaching John would need to begin a new phase in his career building radar installations in Britain and then across mainland Europe. John's battles were over but Gwendoline's (affectionately known as Gwennie) were about to begin.

3

The Battle for Infant Hearing

It is 1972 and Gwennie is asked to address a group of health-care professionals at the Royal Berkshire Hospital about raising a deaf child. The young mother's struggle was a long time ago and there were so many issues. She works on her speech but noisy roadworks distract her concentration. Outside a Thames Water repair crew are using pneumatic drills to uncover a problem in the highway drainage system. Something is preventing the free flow of water. This might be a simple blockage but there could be a deeper problem caused by a breakage in the pipe.

Although she is asked to speak as a mother she wants to use the clinical knowledge she did not have in 1946. She has been testing the hearing of primary school children in thirty schools across Reading for fourteen years and is part of a pioneering team established by West Berkshire Health Authority. The team discovered that around nine percent of five and six year olds suffered hearing loss and were able to organise treatment. Their work challenged the commonly held view that pupils with hearing difficulties were less intelligent. Her thoughts return to the deprivations in the aftermath of World War Two.

The first months of Anthony's life gave no clues to her future struggles. He was a healthy baby whose milestones were normal but as the months passed his limited speech did not improve.

He had developed baby talk up to the age of eighteen months but now his vocabulary was shrinking. At first there was no reason to suspect hearing loss. She was aware of mucous in his ears but found it difficult to convince doctors that this was anything other than a normal infection in toddlers. John was responsible for closing redundant airfields around England and this imposed an itinerant lifestyle on the family. Every move meant registering with a new GP surgery and explaining her concerns to a new doctor. No sooner had she registered with a surgery it seemed John would be redeployed. Then Anthony caught whooping cough. The family were now living in Thaxted, Essex and this meant starting again with another GP practice. Anthony was not seriously ill but she noticed the mucous had turned into a 'brown and evil smelling' discharge. The new GP did not seem unduly concerned and otitis media was diagnosed as the cause of the problem.

Otitis media is an ear infection that can be triggered by a common cold. This can cause a temporary loss of hearing because it prevents the conduction of sound to the cochlea and is known as conductive hearing loss. It is the most common cause of hearing loss in infants and while most infants experience at least one episode of otitis media by their third birthday many will have three or more ear infections within their first three years of life without any permanent damage to normal hearing. The condition is not necessarily painful and can heal quickly. Not surprisingly GPs would not be too concerned. Even if antibiotics had been freely available to rural surgeries in 1949 it would have been unusual for doctors to prescribe them. Anthony was not in pain, there was no fever and he did not show signs of distress. Yet she instinctively suspected a deeper problem. Her challenge was to convince doctors to investigate more deeply at a time of privation. Hidden beneath the surface fluid of otitis media there is indeed a more serious problem; one that the doctors have no reason to suspect. There was nothing to indicate two faulty genes cascading down generations of Lawtons and Shaws to bequeath Anthony the genetic disease, Usher 2. There was no history of deafness in the family. Usher 2 affects the neural transmission of sound to the brain and is known as sensorineural hearing loss. It affects the cochlea and associated structures and accounts for almost complete deafness.

In 1949 she was dealing intuitively with both conductive and sensorineural hearing loss problems that a tranche of doctors had been unable to diagnose. But this is too clinical. She is not a doctor and needs to focus on her struggles as a post-war mother. It was not so long ago that she had endured the Liverpool Blitz and John had survived active service in the Royal Air Force. Unlike millions of people their two lives had been spared. They had been handed a future. She reflects that the Essex GP had made no attempt to test Anthony or refer him to a consultant despite her pleas that her son was deaf.

One evening John arrived home to discover her sobbing as she held Anthony in her arms and took matters into his own hands. He drove them through the night to the RAF base where a young Canadian doctor was on duty. He considered Anthony to be profoundly deaf and arranged for the infant's immediate admission to the nearest hospital some forty minutes' drive away. This confirmed Gwennie's intuitive suspicions. According to her 1972 speech, the parents did not see their son for the next ten days as the ward sister considered family visits disruptive. John and Gwennie had not anticipated their exclusion from the hospital and could only imagine the incomprehensible sense of abandonment felt by a deaf infant isolated in an alien world. Nevertheless following a successful adenoidectomy Anthony's ears were dry and he was discharged a few days later although the lack of hearing would remain a mystery.

A year after giving her speech Gwennie attended an RNID conference where she encountered the ENT surgeon who had removed Anthony's adenoids. He told her that he had detected some residual hearing but was powerless to do anything at the time other than to arrange for Anthony to be examined by Alexander and Irene Ewing in Manchester. The Ewings (later to become Sir Alexander and Lady Irene Ewing) were pioneering new understanding about children who were considered to be profoundly deaf and demonstrated that even the tiniest ability to hear could be used to develop listening and speaking skills. They confirmed that Anthony was partially hearing and advised he be educated at an oral school for the deaf. Gwennie would need to teach Anthony rudimentary speech and lip reading skills at home and Irene Ewing agreed to mentor her. Arrangements were made to admit him to Donnington Lodge Special School for the Deaf in Newbury. It was a new type of oral boarding school, equipped with the latest auditory training equipment. Anthony stepped through their doors in April 1950. The RAF granted John a compassionate posting to the area and the couple, without bothering to view it, agreed to rent a furnished house ten miles from the school in the village of Eastbury in the Lambourn Valley. It was the beginning of a new era.

Prior to moving, Gwennie and Anthony had been making twice weekly visits to the speech clinic at the Infants Hospital in Westminster. Gwennie records it was one of the most trying times of her life because it involved a tedious four-hour round journey for a twenty minute examination. These journeys provoked out-of-character temper tantrums where Anthony would throw himself on the floor of the train kicking and screaming much to the alarm of other passengers. These journeys and future ones to deaf boarding school would be the only times Anthony would express his frustration through rage. Before making the move to Berkshire the couple consulted another ENT surgeon who suggested an alternative plan that involved a fenestration operation.

Another operation? The parents packed their bags and headed for the Royal County.

4

Story of the Deaf

The story of teaching deaf people to communicate was never silent. It is an intertwining saga that begins in a Benedictine monastery in Oña in the province of Burgos, northern Spain. Here in 1584 Pedro, monk and founder of the first school for the deaf, waits patiently for his death. It has been a long time coming but his life has not been wasted. He is at peace because he knows God is infinite and if he tries to possess Him in his limited heart he will fail. A monk must eschew selfish motives. One day he will be regarded as a forerunner of speech education for deaf people. He doesn't think of this now. His mind wanders to the beginning of this vocation . . .

There was once a stranger sitting against the monastery wall; motionless in the relentless midday sun looking haggard and hungry as gusts of wind whip up swirling dust. He feels pity for the man and goes out to him and speaks but the stranger is unresponsive.

'*Entra en la casa y comer la comida es gratis* – come enter the house the food is free' he entreats him pointing to the door. The man remains expressionless. 'It is as if I am speaking a foreign language' the Benedictine reflects. He is distracted by two horses tied to a nearby tree and a dark clad figure running clumsily towards him'

'*El no puede oírlo, señor*'. The stranger shouts excitedly pointing to his master's ears. '*Tampoco puede hablar*' he adds pointing to his mouth. He draws close patting the dust from his clothes, gasping for breath and coughing. 'May I present to you Señor Gaspard Burgos, son of an aristocrat. I am Sancho Morales, his manservant'.

'I was asked to accompany him. He had hoped to join your Order but the Benedictines rejected him because he is a mute and cannot express the Confession – though he is thought a godly man by all who know him.

'I am Pedro Ponce de Leon. A Benedictine – as you can see. I cannot help him enter the Order but perhaps in other ways? He looks like he should eat. Bring him in'.

The dying monk looks with satisfaction at a row of books. The authors are many of the deaf students he had taught and Gaspard Burgos sits amongst them. He thinks of his work with those who had been able to master his finger alphabet for spelling based on monastic sign language. Some learnt simple signing, others limited speech but all had a better future. And so it is that Pedro Ponce de Leon takes his last breath knowing he has inspired others to teach deaf people.

Two sisters from one of the poorest arrondissements municipaux of Paris stand in the snow covered square of the Place de Grève, lost in the gloomy lyricism and solitary crush of the crowd. They wait alongside the unemployed in the forlorn hope of some temporary engagement or, because they are known to be mute, to receive charity. Their inability to hear or speak hides them in the urban vignette and cruel location devoted to the shaming public pillory, gallows and future guillotine. Ignored in their voiceless world the sisters communicate crudely through gestures.

'Nobody likes us'.

'It's because we are a burden.'

'It would be better to run away with the gypsies.'

'They at least know rejection'.

Without work or charity they will return again to the squalor of their neglected arrondissements except this time a visiting cleric of influential means notices how the sisters communicate through gestures. In this moment he is convinced he can help them develop a more sophisticated language and so fulfils his own destiny as he commits himself to the education and salvation of deaf people. The year is 1760.

This story may be apocryphal but it is known that the wealthy Charles Michel de l' Epée (Abbé de l'Epée) opened his house in 14 rue des Moulins, to create a free school for deaf children. He challenged convention by producing a manual alphabet for spelling out words. Everything was based on simple signs, hand gestures and body language to express the French language. Inspired by their progress the Abbé de l'Epée began to teach others eventually establishing the first school for the deaf in 1771. Although it was a Catholic institution with a focus on religious studies the education was free and attracted deaf people from all over France. The Paris institution became a prototype on which schools for the deaf were modelled. The Abbé de l'Epée's rising celebrity attracted eminent visitors and benefactors across Europe including Emperor Joseph II, Louis XVI and the Duke of Penthièvre. In 1791 the National Assembly decided to support the Institution des Sourds de Naissance in honour of his work and to ensure its long term legacy. The Abbé de l'Epée came to believe that sign language was the natural language for deaf people. He had laid a foundation.

In Switzerland another cleric, Johann Conrad Ammon (1669 –1724), had already developed an alternative method of teaching deaf people. His emphasis was on speech rather than sign which became known as Oralism. He believed the breath in speech came from God. If that was his motivation, his practice was to draw attention to the movement of his lips and larynx as he spoke. He would then encourage his pupils to imitate these movements to repeat letters, syllables and words. Ammon was intolerant of the use of sign and so from the outset oral and manual expressions of language were in opposition. Ammon published a book which in a succeeding generation, Samuel Heinicke (1727–1790), would use as a foundation for his approach. He too was also opposed to dependence on sign and attacked the Abbé de l'Epée, in print.

Until the intervention of technology in the 19th century there were no devices to reveal degrees of deafness. People were regarded as deaf or hearing. The invention of the audiometer would later confirm what some specialists had already suspected: that there were gradations. The audiometer enabled practitioners to discover whether it was mild, moderate, severe or profound affecting one or both ears or whether deafness existed from birth or was acquired later. In the twentieth century the advancement of paediatric audiology and teaching deaf people became more closely related spheres of expertise pioneered in Britain by Sir Alexander Ewing and Lady Irene Ewing (formerly Irene Goldsack). They laid the foundations in terms of knowledge and practice in the University of Manchester's Department of

Education for the Deaf; established 15 January 1919. Irene Rosetta Goldsack was well known for pioneering new methods of oral teaching but without the availability of hearing aids she focused much of her work on developing the child's ability to lip read. Her approach was inspired by the belief that speech acquisition needed to be embedded in activities that interested the children rather than follow accepted methods of repeated pronunciation drills. She would further develop this approach with her future husband and collaborator. Together they would advance teaching practice (pedagogy) and scientific understanding of what it means to be deaf to bring a more scholarly foundation to the established principles of teaching deaf people to speak.

In 1928 Alexander Ewing's screening investigations using an audiometer provided scientific proof that children who were regarded as totally deaf had in fact residual hearing. As knowledge and technology advanced it became clear that deaf children were able to respond to sound. The Ewings use of technology to assist speech and language learning strengthened their three core beliefs: the importance of early identification, parental engagement in speech practice in the home and a child-centred approach to teaching that followed the child's interest. The MEDRESCO portable hearing aid was developed by the Ewing's team for the Medical Research Council and made available through the NHS in 1947[1]. It combined expertise in medical, surgical and electro-acoustic technology and education. It is probably the device Anthony would use in his later years at Donnington Lodge although he complained bitterly of its weight due to the large battery. As the century progressed the oral approach continued to benefit from the confluence of science, sensory psychology, linguistics, child development and family support enabling most children to acquire language through listening and attend mainstream schools while dedicated Schools for the Deaf evolved to support children with additional needs.

Anthony's presence in this story occurred later when he would meet one of the Ewing's former students, Dr Daniel Ling, who would spearhead the oral approach in a mainstream primary school in Reading; one of the first to appear outside London. Anthony would join the school the same year that Alexander Ewing would be knighted for services to audiology and deaf education. Alas the Ewings passionate belief in oralism would lead them and Anthony into the full heat of the oralist-manualist debacle.

5

Four-Year Void

Ultimately my days had no meaning.

Anthony is standing beside his mother looking at the imposing mock Jacobean building with its grand proportions on this cold autumn morning in 1950. He is about to start his first term in a special school for the deaf and, apart from a brief stay in hospital, it will be the first experience of leaving the comfortable familiarity of home. A member of staff greets them and they step into the purgatorial gloom of the interior where only his mother hears the echoes of out-of-sight children. They pass a dormitory where he sees a small boy is standing alone on a bed and crying because he has soiled himself. The boy is ignored. The guide leads them into another dormitory where Anthony sees a steel-frame bed. It is a barren prospect. Seven decades later the elderly man has few recollections of four years learning rudimentary speech here. There are no instances of joyful infant discoveries in the Berkshire countryside or of chasing a ball across the school field with other children or the happy bustle of refectory meals. The age of discovery worthy of a thousand days in infant mind-time reduced to a handful of unhappy recollections all sharing the same disturbing emotion of an isolated boy in an alien environment. Four is a vulnerable age to start boarding and fear writes on the chalk-board of his impressionable mind. What shadows did Anthony see passing over the carved panelling in the Great Hall or ascending and descending the Jacobean open-well staircase? The moulded plaster

frieze, inglenook fireplace and rustic light fittings look down to intimi-
date the inner corridors of his imagination and play on his uncertainty.
Anthony will be a weekday boarder but the weekly alternation of his envi-
ronment will only oscillate emotional instability and the experience will
remain with him all his days.

'This sense of distress was freshly triggered at the sight of
the building's familiar elevations when, many years later, I
revisited the school for a special reunion. I thought the effort
might release long buried experiences but it didn't and the former pupils gathered for the event were all strangers to me. The
original school building has long since been demolished and
replaced by a hotel complex. It only exists as an online presence with haunting photographs of happy pupils from 1951 to
1963 – all invisible to my blind eyes[1]. I don't remember much of
my four years here just fragments such as disturbed boys being
toileted before being released to classes at the beginning of the
day. There was one occasion when the school teacher allowed
me to go directly to a class. She said, "Don't worry, off you go."
I was so grateful for that. She was the only teacher I remember
affectionately but I cannot remember her name. I remember her
saying those words. Boys were not allowed to break this rule;
but I was. But I regarded myself a normal boy and shouldn't be
here anyway. What the classes taught I have no idea other than
banging on a table to a rhythm to help boys with learning difficulties remember their names. I had to do this too even though
I knew my name. Ultimately my days had no meaning. They
were filled with this purposeless repetition of banging the table
to the rhythm of 'Ant-on-ee'. These are my only memories after
spending four years at this school.

Donnington Lodge Special School for the Deaf taught pupils to speak rather than learn a sign language. It had been recommended by the Ewings and was a second best option in my mother's mind because she wanted me to attend normal school as a special needs pupil but in 1950 nobody thought in those terms. Had she got her way I wonder how I might have coped? It would not be until 1958 that I would cross the threshold into a normal school and only because the school had a pioneering hybrid teaching unit for the partial hearing. At home the word deaf was scarcely mentioned as I worked through endless speech development exercises prepared by Lady Irene Ewing. I have a vague recollection of my mother's determination. Am I a disabled child in need of rescue or does she see deafness as an aberration – a stigma? She wants me to operate as efficiently as people with hearing – this is her goal. Thankfully in my future work life, I will discover that people who don't have to work as hard as me soften my need to strive but it's my infant years that pay the price. My mother expects effort, effort, effort. No slacking. Keep going. Don't be phased by failures and clumsy encounters. You are normal Anthony. The effort I make only emphasises to me I am in some way not normal.

Donnington Lodge was the only viable option for me in 1950. Teaching styles in mainstream post-war schools would not have made learning possible for a pupil with rudimentary lip reading skills. This was post-war society – rule bound and obedient. There were few facilities for boys like me. Partial hearing means you are deaf. Full stop. No arguments please. In the early fifties people respected the role of 'The Authorities'. If you can't hear you can't easily learn an oral language. How can you lip read if you don't know the words being shaped?

Although I have few memories of this period I remember the weekends at home. The joy of Fridays but Sunday afternoons sparked rage and panic within me. I would try anything to remain, even fighting my parents who found my resistance so exhausting they devised an elaborate hoax to soften the blow. My elder brother Christopher would wear his school uniform to give the impression he was also going to school. The mistaken belief that Christopher was also boarding made me feel happier. But Christopher wasn't boarding. He was attending a normal day school and after the subterfuge had worked Christopher would return home. I still have no idea why my early school years are a blank. There was no abuse as far as is known just the lingering sense that I didn't like being there. It may well have been that limited resources meant a bright boy had to be taught alongside those with more complex needs'.

Interviewed sixty years later, Carole, a former pupil said that she too suffered similar distress with no memories of Donnington Lodge. The case of a young girl displaying identical behaviour to Anthony and Carole was reported in the Wiltshire Times and Trowbridge Advertiser Saturday 21 March 1952. The parents of the child were fined for taking her out of the school and the Secretary of State for Education ordered her return. Donnington Lodge was eventually closed in the early 1960s. A letter from the Ministry of Education to Berkshire Education Authority states the reasons for closure as; the poor condition of the building, the cost of upgrading it and the proximity of St Thomas' School in Basingstoke.

'I was so pleased they closed the school. How did the four-year experience affect me? My attitude was that I'd just get on with life regardless. I remember the other boys being angry. I made the decision to survive these years and I think this prepared me for the trials to come. I didn't have much of a strategy. I was only four. My decision would have life-long consequences because this attitude would feed my fortitude and help me achieve goals but my independence would come at a price making it more difficult to trust others. Donnington Lodge was traumatic as I was an intelligent boy struggling with 70 decibel hearing loss. It was not until I received a hearing aid that my life began to improve. You might imagine what the device was like in the early 1950s: a large box holding a heavy battery contained in a leather holder. I had to wear the device around my neck. A millstone connected by wires to a cumbersome speaker in my ear. Worse than that it was noisy, so noisy it was of little practical use in terms of hearing anything other than a constant crackle that disrupted concentration and made the simplest learning difficult. The device was awkward to use and so in the end I abandoned it. Pointless. It was a useless clumsy encumbrance for a small energetic boy'.

Anthony's uncle is peering through the window into the garden. He is watching Anthony who is six and Christopher who is eleven. He hasn't seen them for some years and the boys have grown. He notices that one of the boys sits motionless on a bench looking at a book while the other rushes around expending great reserves of energy. John notices his brother looking at his sons.

'Anthony has a problem'. He says. 'He is severely deaf'. Cedrick agrees but then John notices that Cedrick is looking at Christopher.

'Christopher is fine' says John. 'It's Anthony who is deaf'.

John is concerned about Anthony's slow progress. Deaf children born to hearing parents get off to a slower start, because unlike deaf parents, hearing parents are not anticipating a problem. These days the NHS recommends parents allow babies to be screened for hearing to avoid a delay in language learning at this crucial time in development. Anthony did not have this advantage. His accelerated learning and new life will not start until the age of nine when he will benefit from a revolutionary approach to helping partially-hearing children to talk. What began in Manchester will be accelerated in a Reading school and the Royal Berkshire Hospital. Anthony's true education started late. Sprinters learn how to leave the starting blocks the moment they hear the gun. They dedicate themselves to this intricate action where the outcome of the race is often decided. He didn't hear the starting gun because he didn't have a hearing aid. By the time most boys were halfway down the track Anthony was still struggling to take his first steps. But life doesn't have to be a sprint – a marathon can provide its own rewards.

It is the winter of 1955 and Anthony is moving to St Thomas' School for Young Deaf Children, in Basingstoke. He will only be here for a few months. The school uses oral and sign methods of teaching. He has the heavy hearing aid that is of limited use and he is known to have some hearing ability. The move out of deaf boarding school nourishes Anthony's fledgling sense of hope. St Thomas' was built a century or more earlier for a different pur-pose. When Hampshire County Council took ownership of the building in the early 1950s it became a School for the Deaf. Here Anthony glimpses the possibility of realising his dream: living a normal life. He can almost touch it but for now it remains tan-talisingly out of reach.

St Thomas' oral methods of teaching are not a strict rule and pupils can use sign. Anthony takes the oral route as his only surviving school report of this era shows. It also reveals his emerging personality. The end-of-term report dated 5 July 1955 states that Anthony is good at dancing and can be proficient at lip reading when he makes the effort. Surprisingly, the report says he has good conversational and reading skills although his written work suffers from a lack of effort. The report shows that Anthony's speech is of good quality having a very natural intonation and good rhythm. Anthony is making progress in arithmetic and religious knowledge. He is also skilful in art and craft classes and loves bright colours.

When the report is read to Anthony nearly seventy years later he is surprised to learn that he liked bright colours. His physical training is reported as 'very good' although it comments that he lacks the necessary concentration for team work. The report signed by Mrs Wilkinson also remarks that 'Anthony's good looks and enchanting personality can be an effective weapon against effort. When concentration can be induced in him, however, Anthony justifies one's faith in him'. Intense concentration would become, ironically, one of Anthony's great attributes as he fought ever deeper challenges.

In his early years Anthony suffered sore throats and painful infections in his middle ear and made several visits to the Ear Nose and Throat (ENT) Department of Royal Berkshire Hospital. He is admitted for another operation; this time to remove tonsils. This second admission would repeat the traumatic experience of his previous stay in an Essex hospital. Again he would be turned inwards to dance with the subconscious; that other worldly awareness where we exist outside of time and are broken and reshaped fragment by fragment.

'I saw other patients in their beds up and down the ward. Some were coughing or talking but I couldn't hear anything because they had taken my hearing aid away. I watched the nurses coming and going busy with chores as if in a silent waltz. Parents weren't allowed to visit children in hospital in the fifties and without my hearing aid I felt alone and vulnerable. I thought 'here we go I've been dumped and left to fend for myself'. I had only recently left Donnington Lodge. I was not happy and then I suffered a breakdown which must have occurred after the operation. I can't remember exact details. But apparently I screamed the place down. How anyone can scream after a tonsils operation seems unlikely but this is what I was told. The nurses couldn't handle me and, once again, an exception was made for my parents to make a hurried visit. When I saw my father enter the ward I sprinted towards him and he lifted me up in his arms and I gripped him tightly. I can only recall this sense of hospital being 'horrific'. But it was one of those fortuitous moments when life changes direction and presents the thing you most ardently desire. Until that moment it seemed my future education would continue in an oral school for the deaf. That was the issue for me. Whether I communicated orally or though sign I would be excluded from mainstream education. Not in my remotest dreams did I imagine my ailing tonsils deflecting the trajectory of my life into a mainstream school. I was in the right place at the right time. I just didn't realise it as I lay in my hospital bed'.

6

Sunrise Reading

'I was about to become a guinea pig along with eight other children. Nobody asked my opinion I just went along with the flow. Reading schools would spearhead Irene Ewing's new techniques in oral teaching of the deaf while the Royal Berkshire Hospital simultaneously advanced clinical practice in paediatric audiology. Reading became a magnet attracting leading people of the day and the Royal Berkshire Hospital (RBH) would produce future innovators and prominent figures'.

During the 1950s Manchester University, University College London and RBH became recognised Centres of Excellence pioneering technology and clinical practice. West Berkshire Education Authority simultaneously spearheaded the experimental Partial-Hearing Units (PHUs) in Reading schools beginning with the George Palmer School in Whitley Wood. Dr Daniel Ling, a former music teacher and one of the Ewings' postgraduate students was appointed in 1954 to head up the programme that would integrate partially-hearing and normally hearing pupils in a mainstream school.

Hospital screening of infants began at RBH after the ENT specialist Mr Hunt-Williams applied to the Nuffield Foundation for funding for a Research and Development project. Funding was approved for a three year research project[1] in 1958 and Dr Kevin Murphy, also a Ewing's protégé, was appointed project leader. The project might not have taken off had it not been for the intervention of Dr David Kendall, another member of Professor Ewing's team. He visited the hospital to allay wide-spread scepticism concerning the ability to reliably test the hearing of the very young. He placated the critics and the project went ahead. Specialised equipment required for this work had yet to be manufactured and so the hospital built its own engineering workshop to build prototypes. The Audiology Department at RBH had been experimenting with acoustic emissions technology during the post war years and its reputation for invention shone brightly when it launched the Linco Bennet Cradle. This was later renamed the Auditory Response Cradle (ARC) and was developed in collaboration with Brunel University. It was the world's first cot designed to screen newborn babies by measuring physiological rather than behavioural responses. Prototypes were issued to twelve hospitals to conduct clinical tests. Four people drove progress; Mike Bennet the inventor, Dr Murphy, Head of Department, Jonny Johnson, a technologist who owned a manufacturing company, Linco Ltd on the Oxford Road, and John Bench, Principal Scientific Officer who through a series of grant applications created a thriving research unit devoted to advancing paediatric audiology[1,2].

The Audiology Department was also widely recognised as an early adopter of new technology such as the Otoacoustic Emissions test invented at UCL by Dr David Kemp as well as Auditory Brainstem Response. When the Auditory Response Cradle was superseded by Visual Reinforcement Audiometry (VRA) Mike Bennet moved to Canada to work with Dr Ling at

McGill University in Montreal but the growing stature of the department began to attract people destined to become prominent names in the future.

At a time when the Ewings' Distraction Test was still widely favoured Dr Murphy risked his reputation by favouring VRA because he realised it was more reliable. His dogged persistence eventually established widespread acceptance of the technology as the physiological test of choice for six month old babies. During the post war years RBH had experimented with warble tone technology and produced the world's first hand-held warble-tone generator for paediatric audiology.

When further funding for the RBH project became difficult to obtain, Dr Murphy lobbied the Government for continued support resulting in the Health Secretary of that time, the future Sir George Godber, helping to secure money for the continuation of the project. Berkshire Education Authority worked in close partnership with the audiology department when it set up the Partial-Hearing Units at the George Palmer School[3]. The Health Secretory for State was so impressed with the progress in Reading he designated the hospital as one of three National Centres of Excellence in paediatric audiology[1]. The department's output attracted international interest and Dr Murphy received invitations to lecture and collaborate worldwide.

There are few records of the collaborative work between RBH and Berkshire Education but there is sufficient evidence to show that collaboration whether formal or informal existed. For example, Dr Ling, the Organising Teacher of the Deaf, wrote in a 1960 Country Borough of Reading Report, *'Today through the close co-operation of education, school health and hospital authorities, provision includes . . .'*[4]. Furthermore, pupils from the Partial-Hearing

Units were regularly sent to RBH to be tested using the latest innovations.

'This new wave of technological progress was only just beginning when I arrived in the children's ward for a tonsillectomy. I had come from Newbury in fear but I would leave in a bubble of excitement – and so would my parents. During my trauma the ENT specialist, Mr Hunt Williams, had told my parents about the new Partial Hearing experimental Unit being set up for teaching deaf children. The unit was led by Dr Daniel Ling who was unknown in the 1950s but would become world famous for his revolutionary methods of teaching partially hearing and profoundly deaf children to listen and speak. He would become one of the founders of Auditory-Verbal Therapy.

I read about this turnaround many years later, in a letter written by my father from Germany. So the man who removed my tonsils was the man who alerted my parents to the forthcoming Partial Hearing Units (now called by the more inclusive term; Resource Spaces) and kick-started RBH's sunrise developments in paediatric audiology. The Reading school experiment had yet to become public knowledge and so my parents were ahead of the curve when they submitted their application.

My mother used the remains of her trust fund to place a £500 deposit on a house in the prosperous suburb of Caversham. The location was important because it would put us in striking distance of George Palmer and enable my elder brother Christopher to attend The Bluecoat School which I would also attend at the appropriate time. My world is harmonious until I am offered an assessment for a place at a prestigious School for the Deaf that is renowned for its academic performance. I don't want this however because it will keep me in deaf culture. The

Partial Hearing Units offer a new approach to oral education in a mainstream school. Fortunately when the day of testing arrives I make a complete mess of the tests'.

The George Palmer School was built between 1904 and 1907. It was dedicated to the co-founder of the world famous biscuit manufacturers Huntley and Palmer – one of Reading's three 'B' traditional employers; (beer, biscuits and bricks). George Palmer School holds a special place in Anthony's heart as he recalls bitter-sweet memories:

'I started at a new school where I met someone who was to transform my life – Daniel Ling. But let me tell you, this was not going to be a bed of roses; he was a strict disciplinarian. This was to be the price of acceptance into the hearing world. I remember seeing him for the first time. He gave me a big smile and I remember the sense of excitement as I looked around the Hearing Unit and instinctively knew I would start to learn now. I hadn't learnt anything up to this point. My life had been a constant frustration. This is the moment real life starts for me. I am nine years old and as my hearing and speech start to improve I am slowly integrating into the mainstream. I simply arrived late.

'Initially I was shocked by Daniel Ling's unrelenting strictness to procedures. Sign language was the enemy. Banned. Woe betide anyone who inadvertently used physical gestures to help clarify spoken language. I remember being caught off-guard when he asked about a fishing trip I had recently enjoyed. As I raised my hands to demonstrate the size of the fish I had caught he slapped my wrists. I was quite shocked but any form of gesturing was a taboo. We all had to learn to speak, listen and lip read. He was preparing us to fit into the hearing world and training our brains to think, listen and speak. You have to speak. The priorities were about talking and listening. He backed up his teaching with harsh reprimands and I didn't always like him. I didn't realise what he was helping me achieve; helping me to talk and listen. I used to complain to my mum 'he's horrible'. But I love him now. Grateful for what he did for me.

'The regime is unrelenting but I am now elated with a life imbued with hope for the future. This is when I learn to talk. Recordings demonstrate how my speech progressed at this time. It was far from clear but I was improving. We were encouraged to attend normal classes with other children. I remember listening to teachers in math and geography classes. Although we spent about 75% of the time in the hearing unit learning to speak it was such an adventure being allowed out to join normal classes. I can't explain how wonderful it felt simply going to a normal school. I was a guinea pig along with eight or more other children, one of the first pupils in the country – in the world probably – attending normal school with a severe hearing impediment. Daniel Ling was later to become famous through his book based on teaching methods for partially deaf children. Parents were warned beforehand that this was an experiment and that it might not work.

There was a risk but not one of them had any hesitation'.

7

Dr Daniel Ling OC

16 March, 1926–9 August, 2003

Kind people often hold the key that allows others to explore bigger horizons. Dr Daniel Ling OC was such a person. 'Danny' as he was known to the Lawton family became a close friend. His working life began in the Signals branch of the RAF during the war years as did Anthony's father although the two never met at that time. The science and technology of acoustics he learned during the war would prove useful when he became a teacher of music. This might have become his life had he not encountered a hearing-impaired pupil and thought 'I can help this child' and so discovered his true vocation. The experience inspired him to undertake post-graduate study at the University of Manchester under Sir Alexander and Lady Irene Ewing.

Ling's future programme of teaching speech to deaf children comprised Lady Ewing's three core principles: hearing technology, speech therapy in the classroom and continuous parental involvement. Parental engagement outside the classroom was absolutely essential to ensure children engaged in conversation in all aspects of family life. The devoted parent however could be exhausting and Anthony later recalls his mother's relentless commitment to perfection, not allowing him to get away with anything. If he mispronounced a word she would make him repeat it again and again until he pronounced the word correctly. Daniel Ling recognised that success in verbal communication depended on constant conversational engagement in the home to consolidate what was being taught in the classroom. This meant talking clearly and listening to the child's intonation. Anthony recalls Daniel Ling when helming a tall ship half way across the Indian Ocean in 2013,

'Even if I had retained some semblance of sight how practical would sign language have been when on night duty at the helm of a tall ship in a stormy sea? Navigation required both hands on the ship's wheel to control the movement of the vessel as it crashed through high waves. With a powerful digital hearing aid I could hear the speaking compass and correct my steering. With the power of speech I could communicate immediately with the crew without the need to take my hands off the wheel. Yes I was deaf and blind but I maintained control of this commercial sailing vessel despite the challenging conditions.

As I felt the sea spray on my face and the sway of the ship throughout the long hours of the night crossing I felt so grateful to my mother for her endurance in enabling me to speak. This above all else made me part of the crew. Yet this gift cost her and me so much emotional energy. A cost my determined mother was prepared to pay all those years ago but learning to speak was at times a tedious business. Daniel Ling was driven by the controversial belief that Deaf schools 'just teach children to be deaf' and was stridently against the teaching of sign language. His entrenched position was later to damage widespread acceptance of his work in the world due to the politicisation of deafness during the 20th century.

I was asked to appear in a film about him many years later. By now I had become blind as well as deaf. The film was titled 'The power of hearing: the story of Dr Daniel Ling'[1]. My appearance did not lead to a career in films but it did in a sense lead to a career on the stage which began in my sixties as I started delivering talks to small audiences on behalf of charities. There is a poignant sequence in the film when a mother speaks of her distress on discovering her young child is deaf and realises, 'My son would never hear me say "I love you". It bought back the recurrent question about the distress my mother must have experienced when in my infant years doctors initially pronounced me profoundly deaf.'

Anthony was deeply moved by the Canadian film. Although it celebrates the triumph of teaching deaf children to speak it opens with a tragic overture; 'one in every 1,000 babies is born deaf. Over 90% of these children are born to hearing parents'. The Reading experiment helped children to speak to their hearing parents and parents to their children. Anthony was one of the hearing unit's first pupils. The approach concentrated on developing listening skills and adapting hearing technology. In 1958 BBC *Panorama* made a programme about the George Palmer Hearing Unit and Eva, who Dr Ling saved from being sent to an asylum, can be seen and heard speaking fluently. Eva died at a young age and Ling honoured her memory when he said 'One learns from one's students just as much as they learn from you'.

He was invited to Canada in 1963 and appointed Professor of Graduate Studies in Aural Habilitation at McGill University in Montreal. In 1973 as principal of the Montreal Oral School he developed auditory based teaching strategies and with his wife, Agnes Ling Phillips, created a parent-infant program. He followed this with a graduate programme in aural habilitation for educators and speech and language pathologists. Later in 1984 he was appointed Dean of the Faculty of Applied Health Sciences at the University of Western Ontario. His academic work and teaching practice enabled him to become a key contributor to a new era in deaf education.

His passion for teaching deaf children to speak was aided by a deep interest in acoustics, love of music and the practical skill to make high quality violins – activities all rooted in his fascination with sound. Dr Ling realised that the logical steps used to train a student to play the violin could equally apply to the development of speech and that hearing-impaired children could be taught to sing in tune through the experience of vibration through their bodies. He later published books about the acoustics of violin making and was the author of numerous research publications and seminal works. He received the Officer of the Order of Canada (OC) from the Canadian Government in 1999 and granted Canadian armorial bearings in 2001.

'When I visited Danny in Canada in the 1970s he introduced me to the parents of a deaf child and then played a recording showing my childhood progress. I remember their reaction. Daniel gave them hope but being taken back to my childhood more than 50 years ago and hearing my imperfect speech was an overwhelming experience and I wanted to weep. It made me realise how much it had improved over the years. How far I had come. I remembered the freedom and joy of being able to participate in wider society without an interpreter'.

Alas the influence of Daniel Ling could not last. He had persuaded Anthony's parents to send him to the local state secondary school where he could continue to monitor his progress in speech. Anthony had wanted to attend the Blue Coat School but his mother agreed with 'Danny' and it was during his second year there that he heard of Ling's departure to Canada.

The advance of hearing technology such as cochlear implants has since enabled even profoundly deaf people to hear. But this is only the first step in learning to speak. In the film Ling says that, 'hearing is not done with the ears but with the brain because sound and language are thoroughly integrated into the nervous system but there is no substitute for hearing...to describe the power of hearing in physiological terms is to say we are neurologically wired to learn speech and spoken language through hearing. It requires different parts of the brain in order to function as a hearing person'.

Daniel Ling's approach to teaching was decades ahead of his time. Although his pioneering work of Auditory Verbal strategies was enabling most hearing-impaired children to receive a normal education his enemies had already drawn the battle line. Forces opposed to oralism sent out a press release denouncing Ling's methods, accusing him of denying deaf children their 'natural' means of communication: sign language. This was published in 1999. The consequences of this political pressure eventually led to the closure of the McGill department.

'Daniel Ling said that 'people who overcome a problem can have an abundance many people are deprived of. In fact more so because they have overcome the problem'. If I hadn't been taught to listen and speak when young what would have become of me? When I became blind I would not have been able to use sign language and if I had not learned to speak what would my life be like? I don't think I would have coped. A nightmare'.

Anthony is meeting old friends, Carole and Barbara. They lip read and talk freely. It is obvious to those sitting at a nearby table that these two women have some distortion in their speech but not that this is caused by their profound deafness. They speak of their experience of George Palmer School, 'There were eleven of us in the Hearing Unit'. Barbara remembers being set a task of writing an essay about the astronaut Uri Gagarin's space flight. She wrote a fictitious story about her own flight into space. Dr Ling was not impressed. He wanted the facts. The frustration Barbara feels when telling this story stirs Anthony to say 'You are a wonderful example of Danny Ling's teaching'. The story reveals the pain felt by a young deaf person struggling to meet her teacher's expectations of communicating as ably as someone with good hearing. 'Danny Ling expected us to learn and do things correctly'.

The women laugh as they recall these distant days with Anthony, 'Girls were better pupils . . . Daniel Ling insisted that we pronounce the sounds of 'oo', 'ee', 'ah', 'm', 's', and 'sh' printed on balloons. They later became known as the 'Ling Six' in honour of his work at George Palmer School and this is now the standard test after fitting cochlear implants. He became part of the advanced guard of teaching speech to deaf children and his methods are taught worldwide. In the end he decided to accept the Canadian Government's invitation because he was unable to advance his work in Britain'.

Carole shows Anthony a journalistic feature from a long defunct magazine entitled *Illustrated*. A young Scottish teacher has moved from a large school for the deaf in Edinburgh to work at the George Palmer School. She is impressed by the speed with which the local education department spearheads this new initiative for teaching deaf children. The magazine quotes her saying 'advances that might take two or three years to 'sell' to local authorities elsewhere seem to be put through in no time here in Reading'.

One of the photographs shows her speaking into a microphone that transmits her voice through a device called the Loop and she is heard on personal headphones worn by pupils within the 'magic circle of sound'. At under a £1000 per installation it is regarded as good value in the late fifties. The previous system would have tied a single pupil and teacher to a desk. The new system frees pupils and teachers for the first time. Other photographs show Dr Ling working with a tape recorder. Secondary education split up the pupils of the Hearing Unit with many of them choosing the oral route.

George Palmer School provides the foundations of speech for Anthony but it is still highly distorted compared to the average child of his age and Daniel Ling is concerned that he should continue to help Anthony as secondary education looms. As the son of a serving officer in the RAF he is entitled to attend the prestigious Bluecoat School in Sonning. This is a place that would ideally suit his physique and ability in sports. Nevertheless he is excited to be going to The Grove School but as he prepares to leave this nurturing environment storm clouds gather on the horizon.

8

One Friday When the World Changed

'If you can't change the circumstances you can change the way you think about them. I was on the cusp of tasting success in mainstream education. I was full of enthusiasm little realising my home life was about to fall apart. My father was a very different man to me. His way was always to quietly dismiss awkward questions and avoid causing pain. He loved his family. Yet on this Friday afternoon the vague sense of betrayal secreted in the words I was about to hear would be beyond my emotional resources. Their implication was completely unexpected as I stood on the threshold of this particular weekend of anticipated fatherly affection.

I refused to question what I was about to be told because I was prospering in the partially-hearing units at school and talking myself into a new existence. It was a journey that had my full cooperation. The ocean current was in my favour and taking me towards the Elysian coastline of my longings. The last thing I needed now was a sea change that would send me off course.

I was ten. Confidence at this age is fragile. Parents help you build it if they themselves can withstand the storm. Overcoming deafness demands so much effort. I wanted my place in the bigger and more dangerous world. But now I was touching danger. I was learning to hear but some things are too painful to hear. Some things you want to avoid facing. Ignorance is bliss when the truth threatens to destroy you. And the truth is that on this special Friday afternoon, arriving home from school at the start of the holidays, tired and drained after a long day of listening and repeating words to the insistent and perfectionist Daniel Ling, I did not have the fortitude to ask the simple question: why?

Perhaps I feared that the explanation was other than presented. Why would I ask for more information if I could not handle it? Anyway, holding a simple conversation with my limited vocabulary and hearing was as much as I could handle at this stage of my life. Going any deeper in trying to understand why the tectonic plates of family relationships were about to move irrevocably was beyond my capacity to reason. I was looking forward to spending time with Dad. His visits throughout the year were rare due to the demands of the RAF so this first night at the start of the school holidays was going to be one of those big seas of joyful emotion and Dad would read me a bedtime story as he used to do every weekend when I was younger. I knew things had changed when I returned home on this special Friday night and heard the words 'Dad has not returned'.

'OK' I thought 'he's not coming home tonight'. The thought of losing just one longed for Friday evening with my father and possibly followed by the weekend without him triggered a deep pain within me and I fought to control my face and hide the anguish within. Perhaps I sensed all was not well. I was Dad's favourite. I didn't choose to be the favourite. I don't think it is a good idea to have favourite children but that's how it was and my brothers never showed any resentment regarding my privileged position in the hierarchy of emotional reward. I was looking forward so much to his return and then in a moment it was taken from me. I assumed it was RAF business and I couldn't understand how the RAF could rob us of one of these precious visits when they had him for the longest parts of the year. Why he only visited occasionally during the year was another question I chose to avoid asking. I arrived home and I remember seeing mum and Christopher, who was fourteen, standing in the kitchen. They were close together but strangely far apart. Years later Christopher would tell me how on his return home he saw mum at the sink with a letter in her hand and staring out of the window.

'I looked at her and she was bowed and looked smaller than normal by some inches'. He told me. The letter simply stated that John was leaving Gwennie and he would not be returning. The shock affected her physical stature. This is what the shock of this unexpected letter did to her and from that Friday onwards whenever speaking of Dad we would never admit that he had left us but simply say that 'he was not coming home'. The euphemism hid some forlorn hope that he might return and all would be fine again. My mother's physical posture suggests she did not suspect her marriage was in difficulty. People can be so blind to things that surround them. Perhaps she knew but was unable to confront a dysfunctional marriage and so let it drift until the inevitable happened and then the end came more abruptly and cruelly than she might have imagined? The wounding was so obvious it led us to becoming a close-knit family protecting and supporting Mum and each other, a band of brothers, so to speak, ready to take on the world. My relationship with Dad up to this moment had been one of reassurance. He provided a sense of security. During my early years I remember him as mild and encouraging. One of my earliest memories was of him making a raft using odd bits of wood and oil drums. He was always making or repairing things'.

Memories of distant childhood vary in intensity. Some survive more vividly than others and are like stepping stones through a life lived a long time ago. Perhaps there is a librarian in the cortex of the mind who busily identifies and selects autobiographical moments that shall prove important to future development and discards the colossal short-term dross that is the essence of unvalued and unlived existence. What remains are the records of archetypal learning experiences. Typical examples might be those moments when the beauty of the natural world or its harshness resonates in the consciousness or the joy of solving a new type of problem. There is an impetus to retain the moment because it is wonderful, important or painful. The librarian classifies and stores them in the memory shelves for future use. As we grow older, the shelves become less populated as familiarity and boredom make mind-time shorter than clock time. The West Berkshire town of Eastbury provided a rich library shelf of memories for Anthony; 'When I was offered a place at Donnington Lodge my parents moved from Thaxted in Essex to the remote and sleepy village of Eastbury ten miles northwest of Newbury in the Lambourn Valley – surrounded by the rolling chalk grasslands of the Berkshire Downs. The River Lambourn runs through the middle of the village dissecting it in two with roads running on either side. The two communities are connected by a series of road and foot bridges. I remember our rented cottage beside the river and nearby bridge. In the 1950s the village was largely built along the banks of the Lambourn. I don't remember people or neighbours from this time. I think we kept ourselves to ourselves. The river was our neighbour. Dad built a raft and Christopher and I watched him float it on the water. He put us aboard and pushed off from the bank using a pole. I remember the sudden wobble as water sploshed against the metal drums and our progress scattering the ducks. There was a ripple on the river whipped up by a light wind and sparkling in the sunlight. Before we knew it we were floating down stream in the central channel. But the River Lambourn is no Thames or Trent. It is a small river littered with boulders and stones. It is not much of a river by river standards and is classified as a winterbourne because it dries out during the summer when rainfall is low. In your eyes it might seem a stream but to a five year old, the sudden awareness of being adrift and surrounded by water, detached from the land for the first time ever, made it feel as wide as the Mississippi.

At this time I discovered the excitement of playing with fire and sooner or later I would find myself in deep trouble. I'm sure psychiatrists would find this compulsion interesting. I don't know why I started playing with fire, perhaps because it's dangerous. Maybe because once it starts it can burn out of control? There's a risk. One day seeing the laundry piled up in the airing cupboard I managed to find a box of matches and set it alight. Woof. Dad's underpants gone in a flash. Thankfully for all our sakes Mum caught me red handed and after she had extinguished the fire turned her attention to me. On another occasion I discovered a candle in a metal holder in a small outhouse. I lit it up like an acolyte performing a ceremonial duty at the altar and watched it burn – mesmerised by the flicking flame. Later I became aware of a black stain on the ceiling and knew sooner or later I would be in trouble. Having failed to burn down the rented cottage, we moved to Newbury to reduce the travelling time to Donnington Lodge. The RAF then posted my father to Germany to work on NATO radar defences during the Cold War and I only saw him on some weekends.

He loved cars and encouraged us to assist him repairing an old Jaguar. We helped with household maintenance. This awakened the left-brain engineer lurking within me. I love mechanical and electrical problems and this ultimately led to my studying engineering at Reading College. Perhaps the most important gift my father gave me was the confidence to take on practical challenges as a life affirming activity. There was no defeat in failure because I never experienced destructive criticism from him or Christopher when we worked together. I remember the time he built a brick outhouse which we used as a coal bunker. We had coal fires in the lounge and kitchen. Years later I was able to take on big challenges such as installing a central heating system and rewiring the house. My father gave me the confidence to think through the problem when I couldn't see the solution. If one approach didn't work I would try a different one. After my parents' divorce, Christopher and I were responsible for maintaining the home and garden. The experience served me well. I am a self-taught plumber, electrician, plasterer, brickie, decorator – amateur tradesperson.

When eventually I realised Dad's absence was permanent it felt like a physical amputation. At least with an amputation doctors provide pain killers to help with the healing. With emotional scars you simply have to overcome or give in to debilitating depression as I was to discover many years later. Progress at school helped to divert my gaze from what I had lost and to look to what I could gain. I had to concentrate on my ambition and this helped to soften the loss of the benign presence I had depended upon. But this weekend we could see we would need to support Mum and that would be Christopher's role. Our world had changed. Christopher was like the so-called 'man of the house'. He saw this as his role because Mum had told him I was disabled and needed to be supported. This was one of only two occasions when she said I had a disability. She also reminded Christopher he had a one-year old baby brother, David. We became a team and Gwennie proved to be quite a leader, strong willed taking the team with her. Just as we were coming to terms with the new order of things our neighbours told Mum that she should go to Germany and plead with Dad to come back. So Gwennie took David and went off to leaving us boys to look after things. She appeared without warning in Mönchengladbach to confront Dad and make him change his mind. It didn't work. She went to Oxford to confront the new woman who she felt had lured Dad away and when this failed and the marriage was at its end, she gave John an ultimatum stating "If you do this, you will never see these boys again". And he didn't until he was in his seventies. Gwennie was a proud woman for whom begging was a demeaning experience but she dearly wanted the marriage to survive. In the end she hated John and remained bitter about him for the rest of her life.

The shared workload of running the house without Dad was demanding. I was just learning to talk but my hearing was poor. Christopher was just starting to prepare for his O Levels having suffered a disruptive education. Life at weekends had been especially good for me during the early years in Caversham when Dad was there. Sometime later he gave Christopher the reconditioned Jaguar saloon for a birthday present. It was a wonderful car; a saloon with a starting handle, spindle wire hubs and sleek winged wheel arches. It looked fabulous and was totally unreliable. Nevertheless that car provided a great escape as Christopher took us on many outings. I remember the early summer evening adventures with the car. The battery and dynamo were particularly useless. If we were driving after sunset we faced the choice of driving in the dark or waiting to follow a car that had working headlights. If we put the headlights on it would flatten the battery. I would shine a torch in the hedgerow as we drove along to ensure we kept our distance. On one occasion the driver's-side front wheel came off because it had been fitted the wrong way. But this was OK. We Lawtons' are quite capable of wobbling along on three wheels.

9

The Grove School

The stage is set. Heroes and villains are assembled. The new boy has rehearsed his part and thought how best to present his character as he prepares for public scrutiny. Once upon a time he was amongst the most physically able in the George Palmer School. Now he is the novice once again needing to learn quickly to survive. It's a gamble. To what extent can past performance or learned behaviour guarantee a positive outcome? Should he slip quietly onto the stage and hide in the hurly burly of the playground or make an entrance; not so confident as to draw unwelcome attention but enough to show he is already familiar with the scene? With distorted speech and limited hearing he will need to be alert to every nuance of change in the dynamic behaviour of the crowd.

When Anthony crossed the threshold of The Grove School he was engulfed by a blizzard of green blazers and red striped ties. This was the chorus line and it included the handful of students who would in some way influence his life. Today he would not be shepherded to the Hearing Unit. Today was freedom day. He would participate in normal hearing classes from the beginning to the end of the day. Every day.

Alas the goal of living a normal life in a normal school would quickly sour. As one of the first hearing-impaired students in a 1960s comprehensive school he was not 'normal' – he was different. Even though his eyes were yet to deteriorate his limited hearing and under-developed speech would mark him out for special attention and leave him vulnerable to callous treatment. He was here because of the influence of Daniel Ling and at his mother's insistence but their enthusiasm blinded them to the social challenges he would face as someone who was always struggling to catch up. Anthony would have preferred joining his brother at The Bluecoat School where more provision might have been made, even if it was only a desk in the front row of the classroom.

'I quickly realised that my impairment marked me as an outsider and challenged my optimism and resolve to succeed in the hearing world. My imperfect speech and difficulty in hearing gave the impression of someone with learning difficulties. It was a prejudice expressed by some and a misconception in others but it amounted to the same thing. It invited torment or pity and there was the relentless stream of mocking jibes and practical jokes from youths whose need to inflict pain arose from their own inadequacies. The psychological bullying became a war of attrition and I came close to losing it. Attempts at friendship generally failed making the few relationships that did succeed precious. One of these was a young person who faced his own health challenges, David Webb.

He was quite ill with a chest inflection. Bronchitis. This caused him to fall behind in his school work and he asked if I could help with logarithms. And that's how the friendship began. I could empathise with him because of his suffering and we became comrades-in-arms battling the horde. Apart from the bullies there were many students who tried to avoid me – which was equally painful. I discovered that David lived near me and we enjoyed cycling.'

The friendship provided a safe space and glimmer of hope against the backdrop of bullying and embarrassment. In 2017 David recalls how Anthony was given the nickname 'Torchy' because of the bulky hearing aid that was clipped to his clothes. This comes as a surprise fifty five years later.

'I don't remember being called Torchy at the Grove. Perhaps after so many years the hearing apparatus had become a familiar part of my life, like a giraffe's neck or camel's hump. I think I was blocking out any unpleasant memories from my childhood. The hearing aid marked me as different when I yearned to be the same'. A giraffe in a field of buffalo. In the midst of this loathing there was a positive experience. 'I had always been good at arithmetic and now I discovered I was good at maths. Maths and numbers are my powerful skills and I was able to help David.

I had good physique and was quite hardy and so the bullying was rarely physical. It was more about verbal abuse and exclusion. I didn't fit in and I longed to retreat to the Deaf world. These days it is standard practice to stream people with disabilities into mainstream schools but I was one of the first and must have seemed peculiar to the other pupils. Daniel Ling told me to persevere and then spoke privately to the Head Teacher who called a meeting of the whole year without me. He explained my condition and told them to treat me as a normal student. There came a time when I realised everyone was being nice to me. I couldn't understand it. Nobody being nasty. Too nice in some cases. Why the change? Nobody had told me about the meeting but if they had I would have suffered painful embarrassment'.

Around this time Anthony made friends with another student who had a markedly different temperament. Trevor was quiet and mild mannered but who nevertheless helped protect

Anthony from psychological forms of bullying and affirmed his sense of self-worth. Trevor showed no interest in school sports although he was a Tottenham Hotspur supporter and to affirm the friendship, Anthony became a follower too, despite the rest of the class supporting Manchester United.

'I had always been very sporting. From an early age teachers had tried to repress my excess energy. I was fidgeting in class and couldn't wait to get out. In fact I was often in trouble for talking and distracting the class because I hadn't heard the teacher speak. Teachers might punish other students for not listening but they could hardly accuse me of not hearing'.

Later David and Anthony made friends with another student, R. They became a noisy trio with mild mannered Trevor on the periphery. Anthony was capable of concentration whenever his interest was engaged and remembers the hours spent in solitude building a stamp collection. Alas there were no Penny Blacks, Australian Inverted Swans or Red Mercurys as the stamps came from the local newsagents. This nascent interest however sparked an interest in geography which would provide his first modest step on the career ladder. Anthony remembers:

'None of us occupied the academic firmament of the Grove, more the undergrowth. Apart from Trevor we were disruptive and thought nothing of running down corridors. Not surprisingly we attracted various forms of punishment, usually lines; writing out the same line a hundred or more times. The predictability of line writing triggered the slumbering entrepreneur within me. When teachers hand out lines, the punishment does not lie in writing lines but in the repetition of the lines. No one ever set a punishment of writing a 300 word essay about why they like to run down corridors. It is deliberately made uncreative because creativity is fun. The Victorians forced prisoners to walk a treadmill rather than to make things to ensure there was no satisfaction in their relentless daily toil – a bit like the mythological Sisyphus and his boulder.

The weakness of this line-writing punishment lay in its nature and since I was given the same punishment so many times I invented a device to hold three pens perfectly spaced for the lines on school writing paper. I was writing three lines simultaneously and nobody ever knew. I could have run down the corridor three times as frequently for the same amount of punishment. I was quite pleased with this success and aimed for a productivity boost with a four-line pen device. Unfortunately this was a pen too far and never worked as reliably.

I joined Caversham lawn tennis club at the age of thirteen. My older brother was already a member as was David Webb and his younger brother Tim who, many years later would become my manager at Thames Water. They were all strong players. My service, ground strokes and footwork were excellent but deterioration in my sight would soon restrict my game.

Friendship with David came with a special and unexpected reward. David's family came from an area near Waterford in southern Ireland and I was often invited to join them on holiday. We took the ferry from Fishguard and stayed with David's aunt Molly who lived 10 miles away from a small and beautiful fishing harbour called Dunmore East. This became a regular treat. We raced our bicycles along country lanes and felt the wind in our faces. I was exuberant not fearing what bruises my restricted vision might inflict as we lean into tight curves and hurtle towards hidden potholes. When I passed my driving test Molly let me drive her car between the house and the harbour.

I remember the joy of driving along the small winding roads close to the hedge row on warm sunny days. One day when enjoying the thrill of driving the realisation of losing my sight filled me with horror. The reality struck home. Suddenly my limited hearing assumed a new importance as it would become my solitary life-line to the mainstream. The arduous effort since the early 1950s would repay a handsome dividend. I had achieved in the past and I would continue to overcome in the future. There was no existentialist crisis even when school life became deeply challenging. My four friendships saw me through it all. The friendship with David was possibly the most important because while the others slowly drifted away David remained. When I reached my early twenties I would introduce him to sailing and we would race competitively for many years to come. But all this was in the future. During the early years at the Grove School I kept a foot-hold in the Deaf world through participation in the Newbury and Reading branches of the 'Deaf and Dumb' Club but I was slowly and surely moving into the hearing world – which although it can hear – doesn't always listen.

10

The Approaching Night

I remember clearly the moment my journey into blindness began. I was sixteen and enjoying a family holiday on the Isle of Wight in 1962. One evening, when the light was fading, we went down to the beach. My mother and brothers were looking out to sea and suddenly became excited. I can't remember what caused their excitement. I felt a chill in the sea air as I gazed out to watch the sun descending the line where the sea meets the sky and realised I had a problem. I decided to wait until the following evening to see if I was simply imagining things. The hours seemed longer that day as I waited for early evening. Everything was fine. Then, at around nine o'clock the sky was darkening and the cause of my fear was confirmed. My brothers had no difficulty seeing the dying light but my vision was black.

'What do I do now?' I thought. What else but face it and move on. I probably knew the truth the night before but needed time to come to terms with this unwelcome discovery. Perhaps I had been hoping throughout that day that I could will my vision to improve. I couldn't. I used to play in the dark without any difficulty but this loss had silently crept upon me. On our return home my mother made an appointment with the GP who referred me to Moorfields Eye Hospital in London. Grey days passed by mechanically as we waited for the day of judgement.

At the hospital we met the consultant who explained that I was suffering from the genetic condition retinitis pigmentosa more commonly known as RP. This would be confirmed as Usher syndrome type 2, a related condition, at the John Radcliffe Eye Hospital fifty-seven years later.

RP is caused by a range of inherited genetic conditions that permanently affect the sufferer's eyesight. Some people lose their sight faster than others. RP attacks the retina, a delicate light-sensitive tissue that converts light into electrical signals that are transmitted by the optic nerve to the brain. Typically these retinal changes cause the gradual loss of side vision leading to tunnel vision and night blindness as well as affecting the central vision. In my case, the consultant at Moorfields estimated that I would be totally blind by the time I was forty. As things turned out I did not need to register as partially-sighted until I was forty-five and could continue to work until nearly sixty when I lost all my useful vision. Nevertheless the Moorfields consultant encouraged me to learn Braille which I tried but found too time consuming.

When the doctor told me I would go blind I remember my emotional response. First there was the shock of having my worst fears confirmed and then quietly but defiantly thinking 'I will just get on with it'. Keep calm and carry on so to speak. But this was bravado. One day I would be deaf, blind and utterly isolated. Imagine my dilemma with only a small amount of hearing and that hearing being dependent on eyesight for lip reading – a skill that only comes with years of practice and effort – and all to no purpose it seemed in this moment. All my resolve and effort to lead a normal life was being snatched away as the Moorfields consultant passed judgement on my eyes. The sense of dread rose within me but this was no time to be incapacitated by fear. 'I've been here before with my ears', I thought. Here I was at the age of sixteen leading a normal life, albeit with a clumsy hearing aid, and in the full flow of the mainstream. So, there was no alternative but get to on with my everyday struggle of hearing and understanding. This challenge would simply become more onerous and require exhausting levels of concentration. But that's OK. Effort brings rewards.

The encouraging thought, if there was much reason to be optimistic at this time, was that blindness would creep upon me gradually. I still had potentially twenty five years of normal life. I could still achieve all that I dreamed of before the curtains finally shut out the light. The years between sixteen and thirty are those high water years of hope, ambition and striving. What is achieved in the here-and-now usually conditions middle age – the plateau of life – and the tertiary autumn of decline. The only difference for me is that the softer light of autumn was casting its sadness now. Dylan Thomas wrote, 'Rage, rage against the dying of the light'. I would do the same in my circumstances.

The reality was that during these years RP did not affect me during the day. My night blindness would only slowly, progressively, deteriorate into an ever more narrowing tunnel of vision during the day over a period of many years. It reminded me of the old television sets of the 1960s which when switched off produced a tiny white spot in the middle of the screen which then disappears in the blink of any eye. There remains nothing but a black screen. But this inheritance was not important now. It waited for me in a foreign land. I was a physically able sixteen year old. I had created friendships with hearing boys and was good at sport. I knew I was bright with an IQ of 138 and already catching up with my able-eared peers. There was everything to play for. Energy was fizzing out of me like a shaken bottle of Corona orangeade. Sixteen year-olds have no concept of forty. That's old. Far away. A place that is not important now. Everything worthwhile is to be experienced today. At sixteen the future is a vast white canvas waiting to be tarnished. It is a place to be explored, savoured and conquered; a place of high adventure because there is little concept of risk. Bad things may happen to other people but not to you. Nothing is insurmountable. Get out of the way. Move on to the next chapter please'.

11

Hall of Mirrors

We inhabit one planet but live in different worlds; worlds of our own making where we try to come to terms with our existence. We do this primarily through our five senses although some neurologists think there are many more all interacting with each other. In 'Eyes of Skin: Architecture and the Senses',[1] Juhani Pallasmaa argues that we use the sense of touch to see through our eyes and without this sensual interaction we would not be so able to make sense of the world around us. Our sight is informed by richer neurological activity. More than sixty years ago Dr Daniel Ling, said 'we hear with our brains not our ears'. It is now understood that all our senses help us relate ourselves to our surroundings. They act as mirrors reflecting experiences that help us recognise or invent our evolving identity. Within this common endeavour deaf people seek to understand what it means to be deaf. Everyone is trying in some way to think about their identity in a world which is not fully comprehensible.

Deafness as an identity may be defined in two ways. The mainstream hearing world tends to understand deafness as a disability in need of medical intervention. The alternative is to regard deafness as an example of human diversity. This approach to deafness evolved during the latter half of the twentieth century with the emergence of publications by academics who themselves were deaf and provided an insight to the world from deaf people's perspective. The publications became influential and helped to articulate the view that profoundly deaf people belonged to an ethnic minority.

Studies of the time argued that self-recognition and recognition by others are central factors that lead to acceptance of ethnicity. Language is arguably the most important way in which a society defines itself and sign language was cited as the more authentic language of deaf people who perceive the world by combining visual and kinaesthetic input. Sign language was therefore the natural way for them to communicate compared to speaking. Ethnicity also requires other factors such as common history and traditions, myth and arts heritage, a sense of solidarity and a commitment within the group as defined by the UN[2] but a common language would arguably be the most important signifier of identity and a nation without borders. It is however clumsy to divide society into deaf and hearing people as there are many levels of hearing or deafness. People with some level of hearing used to be known as Partially Hearing and roughly delineated as profound, severe, moderate or mild. With a 70 decibel hearing loss Anthony was regarded as borderline moderate-to-severe.

The idea of the Deaf world became charged with emotion during the 1980s and 90s leading to a hard demarcation. The two views, deafness as a disability and deafness as an example of human diversity hindered the desire for understanding and was often driven by a sense of injury influenced by an uncomprehending hearing world. In the 1980s and 90s Deaf world activists began to argue controversially that deaf children belonged to their culture. But this was to over simplify the problem; hearing parents of deaf children reacted arguing they had rights too as did deaf parents of hearing children – all had their differing points of view and requirements. Anthony experienced the emerging hostility during his teens in the 1960s.

One cause of conflict was the use of technology. Hearing aids, cochlear implants and other devices were seen as nefarious ways to include deaf children in mainstream life and to deny deaf culture its rightful heirs. The cochlear implant is a prosthetic device that is surgically attached to the skull and inner ear. It enables deaf people to hear. The procedure is usually successful but the ability to hear varies. The implant only provides an electronic sound but with the ability to hear, young people especially, can be taught to speak.

The infant learning process is far deeper and slower than in adults because it involves processes that begin in the womb and is more complex than simply memorising language which is how adults learn. It is now generally understood that new born babies begin to associate the sounds of phonemes and consonants (little sound packets of language), from a prenatal age. Ultimately these associations define the mother tongue. The first year is about listening and learning followed by exercising speech which is first expressed as babble. By nine months a baby can recognise whether a sequence of sound is his or her native language which translates into meaning after the first year of life. Language is therefore more effectively learned at the start of life after which the opportunity for a richer language inheritance is lost. This is why proponents of cochlear implants argued for their early implantation and why the Ewings passionately believed in harnessing children's tiniest ability to hear in order to develop speech.

Today the Informed Choice approach views infant deafness as an ethical rather than purely medical issue and attempts to soften the acrimonious debate by giving parents comprehensive information. The desire is to give parents the ability to make informed decisions relating to the child's future wellbeing. Alas there are no perfect solutions and increasing layers of information can often drive parents back to the specialists for their advice.

12

I Chose My Identity

*'It is not the absence of hearing that isolates people
but the ingress of resentment that poisons the soul.
I had come to recognise that I am resilient.
I am not afraid of tomorrow'.*

'The road to speech began with my mother – she was the tour
de force. She obstinately rejected the view that deafness should
inhibit my freedom to accomplish the everyday things hearing
people achieve. The positive thing to come out of this was my
burgeoning sense that I should expect to live and perform as
well or better than people who hear. The word deaf was scarcely
mentioned at home. Was this denial? I would be expected to
display exemplary performance and I recognise my mother's
stubborn bravery and belief in me; but did she see me as an aberration? The effort I make only emphasises that I am different
and must compensate for this by trying harder than my fully
facilitated peers. In secondary school I have no role models. I am
one of the first partially hearing pupils – a conundrum. Students
do not understand why my speech is distorted. Again I promise
myself that I will not go under. No surrender. Not now at least.
Maybe in fifty years.

My early teens bring me to an early crisis. Recordings of my speech at this time reveal it is grossly distorted and I try to escape the jibes of other pupils by attending the 'Deaf and Dumb Club' near the Royal Berkshire Hospital. I have a deep-seated need to socialise and very few friends. I think the youths of this club will understand my frustrations but they prefer to sign and their hostility to me is no different to that at the Grove school. I am trying to meet the expectations of too many people all of whom have different values and priorities and it is impossible to please everyone. Teenage years are complex. I am becoming an adult and unconsciously transferring allegiance from mother and home to my peer group because their acceptance matters but the process of transformation is a mystery. These are tough metamorphosis years and I suffer strong mood swings and feel restless. My behaviour verges on the antisocial at times. I am lost in the twilight gap between childhood and adulthood.

I need somewhere to shelter from the toxic jibes of school life which seems relentless but this isn't working. I don't really want to be here but the effort of spending all my time in the hearing world is emotionally draining. I know this retreat into the Deaf world is a mistake because I had turned my back on this identity. The word 'dumb' is misunderstood and colloquial language makes it a term of abuse. I know I am intelligent and not lacking or inferior in any group but teenagers are emotionally fragile and sometimes need a safe retreat. I want more support but not the type that breeds dependency. My line of attack is speech but right now this doesn't seem to be working in the hearing world but given my experience amongst deaf people I determine to find my centre and recommit myself to success in the mainstream. I will not capitulate to the prophecy created by others that as a partially hearing person I will always be different'.

Anthony is caught in the emergence of Deaf consciousness. It is militant and he is struggling to come to terms with his own identity: was he a deaf or a hearing person? If he had not been born within a whisper of audible life his attitude towards the Deaf world might have been different. You might think that a limited ability to hear would be a partial blessing but 70 decibel hearing loss left him in a hostile borderland – attacked by the prejudices of the Deaf and Hearing worlds. At the Deaf and Dumb Club he experiences rejection. He thought it would provide a haven from the hostility of the hearing world but his ability to sign is rudimentary. It is no different to inhabiting the hearing world with distorted speech. This is not the retreat he needs. His emotional antenna is alive to the sense of injury that can drive people to seek their own community. But where?

'I could have been a catalyst but it was as if friendship with the one was regarded as polluting the distinctiveness and status of the other at a time when 'the other' had yet to gain acceptance in the world. Militants prefer well-defined lines between definitions of Deaf and Hearing. Ideologues prefer ideology to love; conformity to disparity of opinion. Legitimacy only exists in such a clear demarcation. Some find this world more reassuring but I didn't and I was trying to find my way home – wherever that existed.

Although life in the mainstream is tough I realise that escaping to a minority culture would lead me to a more suffocating environment. I respected those who chose differently because it was about their search for acceptance and acceptance is both precious and precarious. But it is also a two way street. Life for the deaf is not silent. Life for everyone is noisy. Loyalty and betrayal exist everywhere and generate their own emotional noise. Despite the pack-drill efforts of Daniel Ling and my mother I tried to compromise, rejecting their single-minded approach but by now it was proving too difficult. I had been encouraged to focus on speech which excluded sign and I felt I was paying the price.

In the Deaf world it seemed that people with some ability to hear were second-class citizens. Their focus was on the profoundly deaf who were claimed by the Deaf world from birth. Those who had learnt to speak orally were considered to belong to the hearing world and deemed outsiders. There were the profoundly deaf and everyone else. As a consequence I began to participate less in the Deaf social club, missing social outings and other events. Communication is a big issue and marriages between hearing and deaf people can break down through exasperation. The problems are not to be underestimated. Over time my attempt to communicate with people who wanted to remain in the Deaf world became too draining and ultimately futile. I simply drifted away.

Oral communication is constant hard work and at times I resented the effort. I knew the hearing world was stacked against me but I was now a participant and continuing the struggle would enable me to develop deeper levels of concentration and character. I chose to break through the sound barrier. The subsequent struggle in the hearing world began in secondary education where my strange pronunciation of words generated constant ridicule and this would continue into my work life until two major organisations introduced me to a better world'.

Anthony had some speech ability but he lacked confidence. He is adrift on a big ocean. Although he would be excluded from signing with former friends he would swim in the mainstream. 'I could see our future paths diverging. Many years after leaving school I met the parents of a childhood friend. They had rejected the experimental Partial Hearing Units in favour of a more academic route and were taken aback by the fluency of my speech. It was not perfect but improvement would surely come with practice. I was a young adult and this was a cogent experience because although my friend had acquired an impressive array of 'O' and 'A' Level qualifications she was heavily dependent on sign language. It was a powerful moment. I had achieved my goal. I was free'.

13

A Broken Recorder: David's Story

Scattered in open boxes of the school lost property room were pairs of expensive trainers, football boots, leather shoulder bags and cashmere sweaters. 'Whoever lost this stuff can't be bothered to find it' thought David. He remembered an expensive recorder broken a long, long time ago, snapped in two by some mean spirited pupil. His mother would be distressed and he didn't want her to fret. She had taught him to value possessions. 'Kids these days don't need to care', he thought. When David was only a few months old, despite his mother developing a career, life remained a financial strain for a single parent bringing up three boys. The family would endure poor circumstances for several years.

'Gwennie could have remarried and made her life easier' he thought. But it would always be a risk and Gwennie was not a risk taker. Apart from this she cherished her three sons. She would not have wanted to subject them to an unknown fate or unkindness. Was she unkind to them; did she deny them anything important to their development? If so she was oblivious. Her sacrifices, and she made some big ones, were to provide for the family and keep it together. Yet there was an unspoken void. She would not allow the boys to see their father. Was it due to the sense of betrayal and taste of bitterness? Anthony thinks it was probably the best outcome and David believes they all had a happy upbringing without a father. If they had met John as older boys, Christopher and Anthony might have wanted to live a more exciting life in Germany leaving Gwennie and baby David in Caversham.

David's story reveals interesting insights. While Anthony was wrestling with winning acceptance at The Grove School, David was more blissfully attending Caversham Primary. When John received notice of his posting to Germany both parents had agreed that Anthony's special educational needs in England should not be disrupted and that Christopher should not suffer yet another dislocation in his schooling by a family relocation to Mönchengladbach. After the divorce the family received visits from his brother Cedric but there lingered an air of resentment towards the Shaw family. They were not popular and Gwennie was unable to enjoy his friendship whole heartedly. She had never really recovered from the shock of the letter and the possibility that John's long absences in Germany might indicate marital problems and from that moment the family formed a post-letter shield around her.

Anthony took great delight in tormenting his little brother but in a brotherly way of course. He made a bow and arrow which had a pointed tip. He would sneak upon him and whisper 'run'. David knew what to expect and fearing for his life took flight. Anthony would carefully take aim as his brother cunningly zig-zagged his way down the garden but it was useless as Anthony was an acknowledged deadly shot and the arrow would hit the soft flesh of one of David's legs with a sharp sting. Tunnel vision was suspected for Anthony's reliable accuracy. Despite these torments he provided a good role model and did not exclude his younger brother, who followed him everywhere. One favourite game involved throwing apples at each other. No quarter was given to David if he poked his head from behind a tree at the wrong moment. Anthony was also experimenting with flour and water bombs thrown from bedroom windows. The best bomb is a matter of mixing the right amount of flour and water and David provided an ideal guinea pig when absent-mindedly leaving the house by the front door. Brotherly engagements were tough but friendly and despite the shootings and bombings, the youngest brother remembers his childhood as happy, safe and secure. There was an occasion when Gwennie was really angry with him and chased him out of the house. He was running towards the shed for shelter. She threw a table tennis bat from some distance hitting David squarely on the back of his head. Anthony recalls that his little brother was so surprised by the accuracy of the shot he stuck his head out of the shed and yelled 'Bloody hell mum that was a good shot' whereupon she changed from shouting 'I'll kill you' to them laughing about it.

David followed his eldest brother Christopher to the Bluecoat school. Anthony says he associated with the wrong types and achieved little during his first five years. He was encouraged to retake his O levels and discovered the joy of learning. Sadly it was too late to fulfil his true academic potential but he did walk away with five O Levels. During this final year he was appointed a School prefect, captain of the School rugby team and offered an officer training place at Sandhurst with the Blues and Royals Cavalry regiment who were associated with the School. He was a first class shot with an Enfield 301 rifle and a marksman with a .22 calibre rifle. Possession of either of these weapons might have been useful a few years earlier in the garden with Anthony but at seventeen he decided against the army. It was a decision he was later to regret as he recalls 'I would have responded to the discipline. I would also have enjoyed the camaraderie and mum would have been proud of me as an army officer'.

David left Bluecoat in 1973. During his school years David says he has no recollection of Anthony having a disability. Gwennie always treated him as a normal boy and would expect normal standards from him. Perhaps, as a proud woman she struggled to accept the stigma associated with disability that was commonplace in her day and so pushed her son to behave as normally as possible? As his sight deteriorated during his later teenage years Gwennie made no allowances and would not accept excuses. On one occasion David saw Anthony putting a plate on the edge of the dining table and managed to catch it before it could shatter the peace. 'Anthony was never allowed to get away with anything or feel sorry for himself' David recalls. As a consequence Anthony never saw himself as disabled. This gave him an inner belief that he could achieve anything he set his mind to since all his friends were able bodied.

Raising three boys was not easy and Gwennie was frequently annoyed by the consequences of their natural exuberance. She was a single parent trying to contain them, look after the house, cook meals and hold down a career to earn money. It was too much for her even though Christopher provided support and Anthony helped when older. The limitations of single parent-hood did occasionally cause the boys some resentment when they were unable join friends because of household chores but Gwennie never tolerated complaints. If there were problems at school the boys would be more likely to get a clip around the ear than win her sympathy and when things got too much at home she would order them out of the house. A lot of time was spent outdoors.

When Anthony attended the George Palmer School Gwennie and Daniel Ling became good friends. She worked with him testing the hearing of Berkshire school children and this developed as a career. Later he would offer her a role at McGill University in Montreal in Canada but it represented a change that she was not prepared to risk. She met a man named J but held back from marriage and this happened on other occasions. She had opportunities but did not take them. She felt in control and was happy with the status quo. Would a new partner complicate the relationship with her sons? This reluctance would later become a problem for the boys whenever they bought girlfriends home. She could be possessive.

Gwennie was good at networking and in 1973 managed to introduce David to ICI Paints in Slough and from here a career in sales took root. It was in 1972 that the family changed the surname from Shaw to Lawton as part of a means to ease the pain of John leaving and it was an opportunity to continue the illustrious Lawton lineage. During this time Anthony moved to a shared house in Bulmershe Road until he obtained a mortgage for a small flat and found a lodger to help pay it. Christopher meanwhile was far away in India. Gwennie was now in her 60s and moved to a smaller house in Caversham which was more manageable once her sons had moved into their own homes. Later in October that year, following a whirlwind romance, David married his colleague. Alas managing two high-powered careers within a marriage can create unbearable stresses at home and they separated in 1995 and divorced in 1996.

One of the causes of his parents' divorce may have come from

Gennie's extreme caution. As a young child she was cared for a by a nanny and enjoyed the privilege of being chauffeured in a Bentley but when her father increasingly struggled with the family business the home became a place of fear – poisoned by drunken rages. Eventually the business collapsed and even the trust fund set up by her grandfather was plundered. From then on her life became a penurious existence and she counted the pennies learning to value everything – even a son's school recorder.

14

Human Interactions: Christopher's Story

There is a circular scientific instrument known as the Large Hadron Col-
lider (LHC) buried underground at the CERN Laboratory that is so big it
sits across the Franco-Swiss border near Geneva. This is the world's most
powerful particle accelerator.[1] *It uses thousands of super cooled magnets to*
produce complex magnetic fields. They are colder than outer space. These
precisely controlled forces guide two particle beams travelling in opposite
directions into a head-on collision. At the moment of impact new particles
are released to reveal secrets about the universe – and new possibilities.

The trajectories of lives are often influenced by people whose
influence deflect us from an otherwise predictable course. This
might, for example, be a moment of generosity. This was true
for Anthony's elder brother, Christopher, as helpful strangers
appeared on the scene.

'I like to think that these instances came as rewards for his self-
less support when he stepped into the void created by my absent
father'. Anthony said. He was sitting GCE exams and had applied
for management training with the biscuit manufacturer, Huntley
& Palmer and also with Courage Brewery. Huntley & Palmers
rejected him but he received a welcome offer from the brewery.

Then his exam results arrived. Despite his disruptive education we knew he was clever. Now was the moment of truth. It felt at this moment as if his future was in the balance. He needed three O-Level passes. 'Six O Levels' he announced with a broad grin. He had exceeded everyone's expectations including his own'.

Gwennie decided that the brewery was beneath him and with six GCE certificates to his name he should set his sights higher. He had proven his ability in mathematics and science so he should at least think of becoming a chartered engineer. Christopher confessed to his brother that he was deeply relieved. He had only scraped the passes. But as Anthony was to find out five years later there is a world of difference between a grade six and a grade seven. A six presents the world on a plate but a seven takes away the world and the plate. You don't even get the pudding.

But life is often about determination along with the intervention of cruel or kindly people who change your trajectory. A thoughtful neighbour recommended Major & Greenaway, a firm of Quantity Surveyors at 52 Castle Street Reading. Quantity surveying demands strong numerical and financial management skills. A competent QS can minimise the cost of a project whilst protecting the integrity of the structure, ensure statutory building regulations are satisfied and produce a profitability report. Christopher was accepted as a trainee as Anthony recalls:

'I was pleased for Christopher because a job on the Caversham side of Reading would keep him at home and I depended on him as an elder brother and father figure. Major & Greenaway allowed him to attend college in the afternoon. Christopher stayed with the firm for five years gaining Part One of his professional Institute of Quantity Surveyors qualifications. Part One does not confer professional QS status but with Part One completed, George Major signed off Christopher's Articles of Pupillage. I was now in my twenties and David was a young teenager. I was also in the work place with improving career prospects and my mother had established her own reputation in audiology screening. Money was not so tight these days and the family had survived with Christopher's help. He had in fact been indispensable. After five years at Major & Greenaway he was lured away by the prospect of a higher salary. He bought a used Ford Anglia 100E. This was the older side valve, three-gear fifties style model and not the saloon with the iconic cut back roof made famous by 1960s advertising.

My brother soon realised that the extra income came with a price tag. The new firm expected a workhorse who did not want to become a Chartered Quantity Surveyor through a day-release college course. He began to look for alternative employment and eventually secured a placement with the Civil Service who would allow him to study for professional membership of the Royal Institute of Chartered Surveyors (RICS) and then by chance he encountered a director of the Ministry of Public Building & Works (MPBW) in Reading. A year later, having gained Part Two, Christopher was sent to London as a fully charted QS. Gwennie was upset at the thought of Christopher leaving and the trauma of her past resurfaced to trigger new insecurities. She tried to persuade him to stay suggesting he still had responsibilities to his younger brothers one of whom was disabled. But I knew Christopher needed to leave and I took over his role supporting Mum and helping David. He moved to Rodenhurst Road, Clapham. Alas, he was never able to completely cut his ties at this time and would try to juggle two lives by living in London and then driving to Reading on Sunday to help David and me'.

Far away in the Indian subcontinent the threat of border conflict between China and India was looming: a consequence of the failure to adequately resolve the causes of the 1962 Sino-Indian War. These faraway events would affect the direction of Christopher's life as they motivated the British Government to build 'The Nepal East West Highway' in the foothills of the Himalayas in 1969. 'Christopher was sent out as a Cost Engineer responsible for a 50 miles long section of road that joined two other sections built by India and the USA. His middle section needed to span four major rivers. He left in March for a one year tour of duty when I was half way through my Diploma course at Queen Elizabeth College in Leatherhead. In later years he would tell me the story of his journey by train from Delhi to Nepal and his adventures with a German civil engineer and mapping expert, Gerhard Muller, who had been working for the past four years in Bhutwal on a hydro engineering project. Gerhard inspired Christopher with his plans to hike in the Himalayas. He spoke Nepalese fluently and both men were extremely fit and able to walk ten hours a day wearing backpacks.

Christopher would invite Gerhard and his family for drinks and to watch films in the British Expatriates Club. The German family were not welcome visitors and this affected Christopher's popularity too. There were benefits, however, as the family had a car and would take Christopher for day trips around Nepal. When the tour of duty was completed Christopher and Gerhard set off on their Himalayan trek together. Gerard had used the opportunity to map the route for the Nepalese Government. The trek took them through the Annapurna range and into China and Tibet. Crossing the border was forbidden but Gerard knew the lesser known tracks which led them onto the Tibetan plateau. They would enjoy overnight stops in small villages of flat-roofed houses that clung to mountainsides above precipitous cliffs. Sitting in a central courtyard of a family home, they could rest and enjoy the majestic sweep of the mountains. From Pokhara they trekked to the towns of Nandara, Chandracot, Tatopani, Lete and Jomsom. The route then took them north through the ascending Parkhara valley into Tibet passing through the Kali Gandaki River gorge. The ravine plunges between the two mountains of Dhaulagiri to the west and Annapurna in the east to become the world's deepest canyon cut out by water rushing down from the Tibetan plateau. It is a sacred place where the two men would encounter worshippers of Kali and other deities sitting on rocks and in the shallows. These days the famous Annapurna circuit has become littered with the detritus of international tourism and is not quite the lonely, isolated place it was in the 1960s.

After his Tibetan adventure Christopher borrowed a Land Rover and driver and visited Delhi and other places in India before setting off on the long journey home via Japan and Canada in 1970. He stayed with a friend in Vancouver, crossed the continent in three days on the Canadian Pacific Railway, visiting Montreal and Toronto and was reunited with his maternal aunts, Jane and Ellinor. From there he flew home with excess baggage courtesy of Air Canada. He continued his education and gained an MSc at Loughborough University and became a qualified Arbitrator.

Christopher would return to Asia as a member of the Defence Secretariat Overseas responsible for managing all expenditure on building works worldwide for the MOD. His budget would be split between Germany and 'the rest of the World'. The

British Army on the Rhine and the RAF (Germany) spent most of the money while the rest of the World embracing Hong Kong, Cyprus, Gibraltar, Canada, Belize and the Falklands, spent the remainder'.

Anthony imagined Christopher on his first visit to Nepal looking up in wonder at the majestic snow covered Himalayas set against a fresh blue sky. What would it have been like to enjoy that sense of freedom long denied by family responsibilities? 'I thought "he has done all right" as I pictured him walking with Gerhard beside the Kali Gandaki glacial waters cascading down from the high Tibetan plateau. What thoughts occupied him then?'

The Gandaki's progress down the ravine from the high plateau is frequently impeded by rock formations but these are only hindrances. The river changes direction one way and then another as it continues relentlessly towards the tranquillity of the mighty Ganges'.

The Horse

Anthony is standing in a cold field somewhere near Maidenhead.

He has finished setting up heat-sensitive instrumentation that will be used to plan the best route for a new road. It is now late morning and he has already worked his way across several fields plotting the optimal route. He is unaware of a horse on the far side. The horse is a large stallion in a jacket. It is not in good humour. It doesn't want the jacket or to share his field with interlopers who have arrived without so much as a 'by your leave'. Anthony looks up and spots the horse. It is watching him. It is snorting and shaking his head but at least it is on the far side of the field. A colleague is also standing on that side of the field. He is the chainman who assists the surveyor by holding a level rod that Anthony will view through a theodolite – the instrument that enables him to triangulate the position of objects by measuring horizontal and vertical angles.

As Anthony concentrates on the set up procedure the horse becomes curious and begins strolling over. Anthony ignores it. The stroll become a gentle trot. Still Anthony chooses to ignore it. 'If I don't look at the horse it will lose interest and go away', he thinks optimistically. Finally as Anthony completes the setup the horse arrives. It is standing next to him looking down haughtily on someone who is clearly 'town' rather than 'county'. He is interested in what Anthony is doing and stoops to take a closer look. Perhaps he objects to the thought that Anthony might be planning a road through his field. He presses his hairy muzzle next to the *calibrated equipment and snorts steam in the cold winter air. Anthony is not happy. It has taken him a long time to set up this instrument and heat from the horse could spoil the delicate settings. He might have to start over again but only when the horse has moved away. Anthony gently shoves his shoulder into the horse's shoulder. The horse is heavier and isn't going anywhere.*

He tries again this time with more effort but with the same pointless result. No one is giving an inch. It is the horse's field and the stallion feels it is reasonable to investigate what Anthony is doing. The clock is ticking and Anthony becomes impatient pushing the steaming muzzle away from the instrument. The horse is offended. As a quality Hunter he isn't used to being pushed around by strangers. 'Shoo' shouts Anthony and waves his arms dramatically. The horse is alarmed and shudders before turning to leave. Anthony is satisfied with his mastery of the situation until the horse kicks out with his rear leg. It was a particularly well aimed kick. Better than Anthony's aim when chasing his younger brother with a bow and arrow in the garden. The flying hoof hits its mark (whether this was intended or not it is not possible to know) but Anthony drops to the ground in abject pain gasping for breath. Far away on the other side of the field his colleague looks on and doesn't move. He is new to this work and the job description did not mention anything about dangerous animals. The horse moves off and chomps grass while Anthony gingerly pulls himself up the theodolite. He has come a long way since leaving school and it has been a torturous journey to reach this field.

'I was not a star pupil at school and wondered what I would do for a living. Maybe with my physique I could work on a building site or become a skilled tradesman? David Webb was offered an apprenticeship in heating and ventilating engineering. I was pleased for him. You need to be good at maths to do that.

Knowledge of logarithms is useful. I was eighteen. I wanted to impress girls but had few prospects and little to show for secondary education except a GCE Ordinary Level Certificate in Geography. And it was a grade six. Seven is a fail. You wouldn't believe the emotional weight these two juxtaposed grades contain. A six takes you one step forward on the chessboard of life and the endorphins flow while the other confirms your failure. You are going nowhere. What is the margin between success and failure? Six and Seven. I am a success with a six and although I have a 70 decibel hearing loss I can converse.

I can talk and am ambitious. The first career hurdle is modest but it feels immense. At eighteen successful A-level students are preparing for university. I am a late developer due to a delayed school education but I have at least planted an O-level shaped foot on the bottom rung of the career ladder and am about to climb. The next rung will be employment. I am invited to an interview at the Southern Electricity Board regional head office in Reading. I feel excited by the prospect of being interviewed by a big company. The position is for a tracer recording overhead and underground cables. A few days later I receive a letter offering me the job. Although the starting salary isn't particularly high I am pleased and I tell my mother that I will be able to contribute to the housekeeping.

This gives me a sense of responsibility although I am yet to discover the monotony of my future working life. A tracer's lot is a modest one, simply retracing the lines calculated and drawn by a real engineer, but I'm offered the job and am delighted. Proof that I can hack it in the hearing world. It's not much of a job but it means a lot to me today and if you think this is a boring, dead end, Monday-to-Friday existence you are missing the point.

This is another step towards my goal. As a tracer I am in the hearing world and my speech is improving despite my limited vocabulary. I know I can go further than this and progression is only a matter of time and perseverance. I know all about perseverance. I transform tracing from a nine-to-five wage earning existence into an opportunity by enrolling in evening classes. I'm young and full of energy and am not easily tired. After work I attend classes in maths and technical drawing but know better than to try for English. The classes motivate me and give me perspective. I gain two O Levels and am happy but it is a mistake to think I can progress without English. My application for a place on an Ordinary National Certificate course in Mechanical Engineering is rejected at Reading Technical College. English is obligatory. It seems so unfair. I want to be an engineer not a poet. I can talk – what more do you need?

At the Southern Electricity Board my journey into the hearing workplace is lonely. Nobody wants to talk to me. My speech has been improving since the age of thirteen but it is still hard work talking to me. It's like talking to a foreigner. Well almost. You have to listen closely to my distorted pronunciations. If you turn away I have to guess what you are saying and together we produce a dialogue of non-sequiturs. The skilled and unskilled workers are happy to spout colloquial language at me. It's so easy for them because it is familiar, informal and undisciplined. Conversation is transmitted with repetitive phrases. It has all the ease and informality of an armchair. You don't have to try – just let it flow. Know what I mean? Follow my drift? Colloquialisms do not come any easier to me than more formally structured language. All language is hard work. It feels as if I am doomed in their eyes to a life of mediocracy and the indifference hardens my resolve to hide my disabilities as much as possible. Despite the times of feeling isolated it is exciting to mix with adults in the drawing office and my journey into the hearing world is becoming more promising and purposeful. I continue to worry about the diagnosis of retinitis pigmentosa (RP) but at eighteen despite encroaching tunnel vision my sight is not so bad. More than manageable in the mainstream.

The rejection of Reading Technical College is a setback because deficiency in English does not seem so important to the core discipline of mechanical engineering. The failure follows me around for a time like a ghost trying to persuade me that I will always be a lesser person. I feel the anguish of rejection and the fear that I will never quite measure up to normal standards.

I discover that a special college in Leatherhead Surrey is providing courses for people with a disability and I apply for a place on the Diploma course in engineering drawing. Weeks later I receive a letter of acceptance and after five years with the Southern Electricity Board I resign my position. I am doubly excited because before starting the autumn term I have an outdoor adventure holiday to enjoy. It includes all sorts of activities such as horse riding, canoeing, rambling and climbing. I enjoy the varied experience apart from horse riding. This is when I first suspect horses don't like me. I am happy waddling along on an old cob but it doesn't seem to respond to the control mechanisms. I can neither increase its speed nor stop it – so we waddle safely onwards until we come to a farm gate that is partly open. I can see that while there might be room for the horse to get through there doesn't appear room for two legs: one on either side of the saddle. The hand brake and footbrake continue to have no effect and I watch the narrow opening waddling towards us. Suddenly

I realise that my right leg is snagged on the gate and my left foot is trapped in the stirrup and I am slowly being waddled out of the saddle. I worry about my anatomy. Thankfully as we reach the tensile limits of orthopaedic construction my foot releases itself from the stirrup and I fall to the ground. The horse stops and looks back disdainfully. Nasty horse.

The Queen Elizabeth Foundation helps people with disabilities to lead more independent lives. The people I meet here suffer all sorts of disability but mostly physical ones. The course in Leatherhead means I need to board but this is a relief as home life with my mother is becoming more difficult. The Diploma is a nine-month course in engineering drawing and I check in advance that Reading Technical College will accept it for entry onto the Ordinary National Certificate (ONC) course. The Queen Elizabeth Foundation is an unexpectedly helpful experience. It not only provides an academic bridge but helps with my social skills too but at the end of the course, controversially perhaps, I am happy to leave as in some ways it seems to be taking me back into the world I am trying to escape.

On returning to Reading I quickly find a new job with an engineering company, Jig & Tool Design Limited, located close to the Royal Berkshire Hospital. I reapply to Reading Technical College to do ONC without English and they accept my application for this two-year day release course. As the first day of college looms I become increasingly anxious because this is a new experience. I wonder how the other students will treat me once they discover I am deaf. This will become evident the moment anyone tries to speak to me in a noisy cafeteria or corridor.

I am well into the course when I am made redundant from J&T Design. I don't know why and am confused. I felt confident in my general performance in the workplace. It may be due to the company losing a major contract or becoming less profitable but two employees have to go and I am one of them. I hear about an opportunity in Berkshire County Council's Highways Department and obtain an interview at the Council's offices. In the past employers viewed hearing as a disability and exercised caution believing that lack of hearing equated to lack of intelligence. Perhaps they think it will take a lot more effort to explain things to a deaf person? More time required to fulfil every minor task? My suspicions are justified.

One of the interviewers explains sympathetically that they are not sure about my ability to do the job but announce they were willing to allow some leeway in the form of a six months trial as a draftsman in the Department of Road and Footpaths. I will have the title of a Junior Civil Engineering Technician. My line manager seems accomplished and from the moment I start I watch and listen intensely to ensure I compensate for any frustrations my limited hearing might cause. I will prove that lack of hearing does not require leeway. My previous jobs had been monotonous but here is something worth learning. I am so relieved to get my foot in the door even though every day of the trial colleagues are monitoring and assessing my ability to cope but I was always a keen and enthusiastic worker. Positive. These colleagues are lovely intelligent people and willing to help with daily tasks.

I feel close to my goal of being offered the full time post but it is not yet certain although I know my work is respected and I am popular. I enjoy the challenges of roads and footpath design and surveying. I particularly like the field work although I did learn to respect horses. I complete the trial and am offered a permanent position. At college I switch from Mechanical Engineering to Civil Engineering and excel in physics and maths, especially applied maths, but English remains difficult. Nevertheless after four years I am promoted to senior civil engineering technician. I enjoy the outdoor surveying work using an analogue theodolite for measuring horizontal and vertical planes and then manually calculating positions.

The effort of sustaining my concentration on any task would lead to promotion but this was not my primary motivation. I need this level of concentration to ensure I talk correctly and not draw attention to my hearing. When I struggled to speak at school, Daniel Ling would tell me to write it down first and then read it. But what I wrote down was always different to what I wanted to say. Is this dyslexia? It was weird.

During these years I was allowed to attend college one day a week and succeeded in gaining the Ordinary National Certificate (ONC) – the prize I had waited so long to win. It was also a confirmation that the Queen Elizabeth College Diploma had indeed enabled me to cross the bridge to mainstream opportunity. The Higher National Certificate in Civil Engineering followed although knowledge acquisition continued to be a trial as I needed to fill the gaps whenever lecturers turned their heads away. Nevertheless I passed the exam by carefully selecting questions based on calculation rather than written answers. In the workplace I would always struggle writing reports.

Once I had gained the HNC qualification I stopped. I always knew I would stop at HNC because this would be sufficient to support a career in engineering. I would have prepared for professional qualifications if I thought my eyesight would endure beyond forty. With hindsight I made the right choice. Who would have thought in the early 1970s that, forty five years later, a front page story in *The Times*[1] would report private schools encouraging students to gain vocational qualifications in subjects such as engineering, construction and agriculture rather than follow the traditional university route? Really? I could have told them that. If you want able minded people in the workplace employ a disabled person who has already achieved against the odds.

These are good years for me as I am more fully accepted by colleagues but conversations in noisy areas are a challenge and at times gruellingly unpleasant as I desperately try to focus on what is being said. This is the price I pay for being part of the hearing world. I am talking and listening and it feels precious. Despite my academic achievement the daily effort required to engage in conversation is tiring but it strengthens my powers of concentration. Qualifications and training are essential for the workplace but I need more than this for a fulfilling life. I did not gain A Levels at school but I did learn to talk, hold a conversation and have a moderate ability to write. Have you ever thought how you learned to read and write? It requires two independent but related capabilities. You need to have some familiarity with language. This most naturally comes from infant conversations with your parents and then making the connections between sounds and printed words[2]. Babble leads to nursery school teachers pointing to pictures of cats and spelling the word as it is spoken phonetically.

Unfortunately as my career prospects are becoming more promising my relationship with my mother is deteriorating again. I realise now that she never really overcame the traumas of her childhood and the shock of my father leaving. And so my probing questions and desire to rekindle contact with him a decade or so after the divorce are not helpful. I don't know what she is thinking but she considers any attempt to meet my father as an act of betrayal. Home life has become painful and I spend more time playing tennis'.

Not far from the tennis club a pleasure craft disturbs a grey heron on the banks of the River Thames. It takes flight and then descends precariously towards the water before lifting gracefully into the air. The bird's movements that seemed so awkward at first now become smoother as it gains altitude and eventually flies rhythmically into the late morning light – disappearing above the trees.

16

The River Odyssey

Concerns for adequately meeting the demand for water in London and managing its sanitation have tasked the minds of establishment figures since the early 1600s. Incessant population growth and its associated economic activity continually threatened to overwhelm whatever infrastructure was put in place. The industrial revolution and the Big Stink of 1858 provided two noteworthy wake-up calls. These concerns have since echoed in the boardrooms of regional water authorities surrounding the capital. One important source is the River Thames and the endeavour to improve supply here would one day conjoin with Anthony's concern to advance his career and income.

During the 1960s Anthony was oblivious of these problems as he noisily worked on his geography O level. Synchronicity is a wonderful thing and this O level would prove useful in later life as would the endeavours of the local Scout movement meeting at nearby St Andrews Church. There in the timbered interiors of the Scout hut and environs of south Oxfordshire Scout leaders busily taught him map reading skills whilst moulding him into a responsible future citizen of the United Kingdom. Meanwhile across the river various water harvesting schemes were being considered in the HQ of Thames Water. One idea was to collect

untapped water naturally stored in chalk aquifers in low population areas of South East England.

During the years from 1967 to 1970 a tributary of the Lambourn River was identified as being suitable for a pilot study to
see if this strategy would work. The plan was to direct groundwater from the chalk aquifer during times of drought and
direct it to London using the existing River Kennet and River
Thames. An initial pilot study was successfully undertaken and
The Thames Groundwater Scheme was born. A network of large
abstraction and observation boreholes together with pipelines
and control equipment were installed throughout the Lambourn and related river catchments. This produced a cascading
network of pipes and streams that would gather the water and
so increase its availability to the capital.

The water would never run out because the plan allowed for
depleted aquifers to be replenished during the winter or during
times of unusually heavy rainfall. Unfortunately completion of
the project coincided with the most serious drought in 50 years
in 1976. The increase in river flow was subsequently found to
be too small to benefit the capital and the project was shelved
although the distribution network was retained for future use
and renamed the West Berkshire Groundwater Scheme.

The network would need to be maintained and monitored
and this would require regular flow measurements to be taken
by hydrometric technicians on an almost daily basis. Knowledge
of geography and good map reading skills would be useful to
this work as would a dependable car. An interest in maths would
also be useful for making accurate forecasts. The data collected
by technicians would subsequently be archived at the Thames
Water HQ in Reading and made available to any organisation

requiring it such as the Meteorological Office or civil engineering companies needing to be aware of river behaviour.

The gathering and processing of this aquifer data would become Anthony's world and he would love one part of the work and live in fear of the other – but he had yet to apply for the job. His river odyssey began in 1975 with a Thames Water recruitment advertisement for hydrometric technicians. Anthony optimistically submitted his job application. He had been promoted to Senior Civil Engineering Technician at Berkshire County Council. 'This was real engineering,' he proudly professed but after many years it was time for a change. The work of designing and building roads and footpaths was becoming familiar and he wanted to try something different. Thames Water invited him to an interview where it was explained that the management of water resources and ability to forecast flooding and river behaviour was wholly dependent on the quality of data collected and processed by hydrometric technicians. Accuracy was everything. These technicians spent a lot of their time literally in the field, searching for water gauges and bore holes where they would collect data by measuring ground and surface water. The River Thames flows 184 miles from its source in the Gloucestershire Cotswolds to the Thames estuary where it is swallowed up in the North Sea. This would appeal to Anthony's sense of adventure.

Car ownership was a necessary requirement and when pressed on the quality of his aging MGB sports car, Anthony assured the interviewer that although it was old it was in better condition than many younger vehicles because he maintained it meticulously. He was thrilled to be offered the job. Had Mrs Wilkinson, his old Basingstoke school teacher been present, she might have told him that it was his personality as much as his experience and

HNC that had got him through. This was the year Rod Stewart launched his landmark song 'Sailing'. It became Anthony's favourite melody but it is not about sailing or ships as Anthony thought but about our mysterious journey through life. At least this was the intention of the song writer Gavin Sutherland. Anthony associated it with this happy moment in his life but it would become a bitter-sweet lament his daughter, Sarah, would recall many years later on a racing yacht in Sydney harbour. She remembered the sadness of her parents' divorce. She had seen the silent tears he thought he was hiding whenever the song was played.

Anthony joined the hydrometric department during the summer of 1975 and was assigned to the surface water team. The field work would return him to the playground of his infancy and the gently sloping chalk uplands of the Lambourn Downs that stretch between the Ridgeway to the north and the River Kennet to the south. This rolling open vista would become his haven. The upper valley of the River Lambourn in this land of Egypt would offer rich solitude to a man escaping the plagues of his youth. This chalky landscape with its wide vistas and wild winds offers poor grazing to farmers but it would be no desert experience for a man finally set free from bondage. A chalk aquafer fed by a stream, also known as a bourne, begins in these uplands and Anthony would spend many years monitoring its flow through this westernmost part of Berkshire squeezed between the boundaries of north-east Wiltshire and south-west Oxfordshire.

Many of his days would be spent in waders taking measurements with a current meter or collecting ground and surface water data. This would be enjoyable employment for an outdoors man but the River Thames in full flood is an unforgiving environment and in the 1970s and 1980s collecting data from water gauges could be dangerous work. Technicians worked alone, often in remote places and precarious conditions. The dangers increased when technicians working in isolation changed their work schedule without notifying the office. This meant they would be listed in the wrong place if they were reported missing. First generation mobile phones were issued to technicians but they were bulky and lone river workers tended to find themselves outside signal spots. Sometimes risks were exacerbated by bravado. One colleague confessed that to read a meter inaccessibly located under a bridge he needed to walk sideways along a thin concrete wall submerged by fast-flowing flood water. He could have slipped but having arrived at the destination he was determined to obtain the reading. This was the spirit of the team Anthony had joined.

Having secured a position in the gilded halls of the corporate mainstream Anthony did not talk about his physical limitations as by now his speech was much improved. He had passed through the net unnoticed. What would he gain from unnecessary confession other than to risk having his cherished accomplishment taken from him? These were halcyon years as Anthony roamed the Thames Valley in his beloved sports car looking for wells and bore holes buried in fields of tall grass and water gauges obscured by undergrowth. He was never happier than when overcoming the challenge of finding these remote measuring stations – even when up to his knees in mud. Some technicians drove unnecessary distances to find them usually because they could not read a map correctly. There are approximately 1,000 wells that need monitoring across the Thames Valley. Some are big and others small, some are monitored monthly others every six months or annually. Without experience it is like finding the proverbial needle in a haystack but they had to be found and a reading obtained. Anthony was renowned for his ability to find them along with his proficiency with maps.

This was Anthony's life at Thames Water and though he roamed freely through the Thames Valley he lived in a world of blurred edges that framed his vision. Without peripheral sight he needed to frequently scan the horizon for hazards rather like a field mouse alert to the possible presence of a predator or a trap. He knew time was not on his side and failing sight would force retirement. This happened in 2003. From the day he joined Anthony could see it coming. It was just a matter of time; a hundred thousand squints measured out in years.

For the time being, however, the Thames Valley countryside provided a work haven for a man hiding an inconvenient secret from colleagues. Here in all weathers whether driving through snow drifts on the Ridgeway or searching through summer undergrowth for hidden water gauges at the river's edge Anthony was free to be himself and live with his minor accidents out of sight of prying eyes. As long as his data was good he could be his own boss in control of all he surveyed. What did kingfishers care about his lack of sight or hearing? Water voles scampered around the water's edge as he stumbled by in sloshing waders; not for him the angler's displeasure of hearing provocative gulps of roach and ruffe as they defy capture.

The inevitable happened during a team project one warm peaceful summer morning. It was a blissful day in so many ways when Anthony and his colleagues arrived at the river's edge in Windsor Great Park. The Thames was in full flood and their mission was to measure the speed of water flow. It was a familiar procedure and they began by fixing a safety line with red warning flags across the river using an open boat called a dory. They then traversed the river taking measurements at regular intervals. The readings would be used to calibrate a new riverside ultrasonic gauging station which will automate the production of future hydrographs that reveal river behaviour throughout the year. Ironically the new installation will remove much of the danger of data collection that Anthony thrives upon.

Forecasting is a statutory duty but Anthony doesn't think in terms of strategic responsibilities today as he surveys the angry river glistening in the sunlight. He is simply looking forward to another adventure on a small boat. This vision is shattered when the team leader hands him a megaphone and tells him to stay on the riverbank as lookout. Anthony is not the ideal candidate for lookout but no one knows about the severity of his tunnel vision and he isn't about to tell them. Although the river has been closed to traffic his purpose is to warn off unsuspecting boats approaching the line oblivious of the danger. The river is swirling with powerfully interlacing currents. As he peers into the disturbed surface he sees watery serpents rise up only to be sucked under again as fierce currents entangle themselves and he understands how swollen rivers swallow cavalier swimmers. His imagination soaks up long laborious minutes. As the hours pass Anthony fights boredom just as his father had done in the Signals office of RAF Hucknall below the empty skies of 1939 as he waited for silent tele printers to burst into life declaring the start of World War II.

Anthony's responsibility today is to scan the empty river for approaching boats. It is a blissfully quiet summer's day until he notices his colleagues shouting and waving frantically from the dory. He turns to scan the river and sees the fast current driving a boat towards the cable. He reaches for the megaphone to amplify his anxious warning. Fortunately the helm is a competent local and completes a u-turn without creating an incident. The danger passes, his colleagues stop panicking and work is resumed until the team leader falls out of the dory into the river. He has never done this before. The strong current pushes him against the high side of the boat. He manages to grab the safety cable and manoeuvre his body against the force of the water to reach the stern where it is easier to clamber aboard but the inflated lifejacket makes it difficult to move. His colleague is telling him to pull himself up but the team leader is becoming cold and tired. Slowly his grip on the cable weakens and as he feels his strength leaving his fingers other hands slip under his shoulder to hoist him aboard.

Two potential tragedies have been averted and the boat is steered towards the opposite bank to collect Anthony. The safety cable is wound in and the dory heads for the boathouse. As they approach the slipway Anthony, who is the most experienced boat handler of the four, takes the wheel. While the team leader remains slumped wet and cold one of Anthony's other colleague's stands near the bow ready to jump onto the approaching slipway. Unfortunately as Anthony concentrates on the mooring he fails to see the dark relic of a dead tree protruding from the water on the periphery of his vision. He runs into it catapulting his colleague into shallow muddy water where he sits cursing him enthusiastically. The incident is subsequently investigated by a Health and Safety officer whose report shows that despite the accidents the team had followed procedures sensibly. No mention was made of Anthony's limited eyesight, which continued to be a cherished secret.

17

Working within Walls

In the 1970s before telemetric systems could transmit data from remote riverside devices to office computers, Anthony felt more secure when battling riverside hazards than processing data in a busy office. But harvesting data from the fields was only half the responsibility of a hydrometric technician. It was in the office that Anthony felt most vulnerable as he juggled conversations, interjections, oral requests and telephone questions while interpreting the language and guessing the meaning in a noisy open-plan milieu of loud voices and humming machines. Did he really think he could hide his inability to hear or see clearly? This was the fear he lived with, had lived with but more so now having secured the ideal career. He thought his bluff was working but it was obvious to a sympathetic colleague that Anthony struggled with the noise of cross conversations.

'I would be on the telephone and have to pick up key words to imagine what was being said. And I would say 'yes', yes, I see' and hope they believed I understood. I would then have to find out what the call was about and what I was to do. Sometimes this landed me in deep trouble but often I was able to 'wing it' with the support of this colleague. She had a strong clear voice and was always happy to help with written reports and other documentation that required the dreaded use of English'.

The colleague had joined the hydrometric team after noticing its upbeat character and realised she would prefer working outdoors rather than at a desk in financial management. Anthony remembers that although she was the sole woman in the team she was treated as one of the 'boys' because she worked alone and shared the same risks and discomforts.

She recalled that while colleagues were aware of Anthony's minor speech impediment no one appreciated how limited Anthony's sight was becoming. They were simply impressed by his ability to complete tasks and his expertise in Computer-Aided-Drawing (CAD). They also noted his indifference to anything happening around him. Perhaps it was a consequence of maintaining a subterfuge that he would rarely ask others for help and refused to be defeated by technical challenges. If he failed he would simply try a different approach until the problem was solved. Colleagues knew that when he promised to do something it would be done effectively. His powers of concentration combined with a 'happy-go-lucky' persona made him an endearing member of the team.

'I did my best to disguise limited vision. It was like looking through a periscope and I was the skipper of a submarine in dangerous territory trying to avoid scrutiny. Every time I enter the premises I remind myself to avoid unnecessary collisions or display other forms of clumsiness. Whenever I need to leave my workstation I raise the periscope in search of potential hazards.

'Brain to eyes up periscope'.

'Periscope to brain; what is that on the floor?'

'Brain to neck; stop turning neck your behaviour will raise suspicion'.

'I feign 20/20 vision by disguising the need to move my head more than most people but I must look more carefully where I am walking. Miss-firing ears are enough in this busy place'.

With hindsight Anthony was blessed with belonging to a small group that survived numerous management transformations and corporate takeovers. The team was never disbanded and the ties of loyalty endured. Anthony believes their survival was due to the group's data collection work being essential to the hierarchy of successive regimes whether under the banner of Thames Water, the National Rivers Authority or the Environment Agency. While other groups were dissolved the hydrometric team blissfully glided along like an old carp escaping the hook. There was no destructive competition amongst them. They were a happy team. The bond of loyalty increased throughout this era of uncertainty as the group survived successive swathes of reorganisation and although the hydrometric group was shuffled around, unlike other groups, individuals were never required to reapply for their own jobs. The team manager recalled that they 'were lucky'.

Anthony's failing sight however was beginning to risk more serious consequences. His sympathetic colleague began to suspect a problem when following him on the M25. He was towing a boat with an outboard engine when the cowling blew off the outboard. It flew into the air and hit the Land Rover she was driving. She pulled over but Anthony continued without realising what had happened. Her suspicions were confirmed when on one occasion she noticed his head constantly moving to scan the road ahead. She became concerned and asked 'be honest with me Anthony, what can you see?' If worry provoked the question his answer gave grounds for deeper concern. His sight was far worse than she imagined and it raised a question about road safety since the work of a hydrometric technician involved so much driving. Matters came to a head on another occasion when someone carelessly opened the door of a parked car just as Anthony was passing and he hit it. No one was injured but it distressed him until the other driver emerged apologetically. Although it was not his fault Anthony realised the seriousness of his continuing on the road. He was at the tipping point of quitting and just needed someone to nudge him into making the decision. Anthony says,

'My car was an essential part of my life. I was already divorced and if I couldn't drive I would lose my job and a large chunk of my identity would be taken away. I was not ready for this'.

It was obvious that he needed to confront his deep psychological need to drive – this symbol of living a normal life. Except this wasn't normal and he knew it. Eventually he arranged a meeting with his manager to explain that his vision was now severely limited.

'How much can you see?' The manager asked.

'I can see you. But you are in a box. I can't see anything around you.'

The manager was horrified to realise the extreme limitations of his vision. It was far worse than he imagined and said 'thank goodness you want to stop driving because we were all becoming concerned'.

'I need this job' Anthony pleaded in desperation to keep hold of his lifeline to the mainstream. He thought an inability to drive would deprive him of a role in the workplace and this raised the spectre he so feared: loneliness and isolation. He had put so much emotional effort into this journey but had he simply built a house of cards? It would feel like surrender and he was afraid. His manager reassured him. Thames Water, which some years ago had become The National Rivers Authority was now part of the Environment Agency. As a large public sector organisation it needed to show it had an inclusive employment policy. Anthony simply needed to register as disabled and he would be far less likely to face redundancy at a time when serial reorganisation was leading to job losses. 'Everyone else needs to worry about their job but you have a job for life' he said bluntly.

He found Anthony the perfect office-based role with a new responsibility for data validation and quality assurance. Searching the Berkshire Downs for water meters was now clearly over but Anthony remembers that one of his proudest achievements of that era was his responsibility for managing the rainfall network and installing ultrasound gauging stations. Eventually the department was disbanded and moved to Hatfield, Frimley and Wallingford which were all difficult to reach without a car. This was the beginning of the end. Without a car he was stuck.

An offer of redundancy was offered and politely refused and the potential impasse was resolved when someone managed to reassign him to the hydrology department. The new head of department was sympathetic to Anthony and determined to help him. The team consisted of people who specialised in mathematical modelling and the move played to Anthony's mathematical strengths. Once again he had found himself a new challenge in a stimulating environment. This was to prove a fitting end to his working life. Anthony recalls, 'I missed my friends in hydrometrics but the next six years were to become the most fulfilling in my water management career'. Despite his commitment to the new role his age, limited hearing and fading sight made the work exhausting. Tunnel vision had not initially affected his ability to focus on a computer screen but even this lifeline was now failing him as was his ability to read. He felt guilty and even ashamed of the mistakes now creeping into his calculations.

'I always wanted to do my best but it felt as if the workplace had put me on the frontline of a war zone. Perhaps I was succumbing to anxiety because at the end of every day it felt as if I was fighting to survive simply to work another day. I realised this was the end of my career years and eventually I requested early retirement. I was given an independent assessment but no alternative opportunity was found. I was just 58. I would have liked to have reached my 60th birthday before retiring but I simply couldn't continue. All the years of bluff and bluster were over. I no longer had any need to conceal my disabilities. Now I could relax. Ho ho'.

During the intervening years the work of a field-based hydrometric technician had changed. It had become more administrative with many tasks considered too dangerous for lone workers. Technicians now measure river flow using drones and mobile phones rather than hanging out of boats holding a propeller attached to a long pole. Perhaps the blessing for Anthony was that he was born in an analogue age before digital technology could rob him of adventure beside turbulent waters.

'Could my work life have been easier?' It is only when Anthony admits to the severity of his dual sensory loss that he realises, for the second time in his life, he is finally free. Free from having to hide the truth. Free from constantly readjusting to hide his changing limitations. Free from the fear that his disabilities made him a lesser person. There was nothing to hide anymore. A secret that was never a guilty one but became one.

He was finally free of the captivity of working within walls. Walls that he made.

18

Social Eyes

The journey into my second marriage began when I registered as partially sighted. I was still working at this time but no longer driving. Social Services provided training with a long red-and-white cane which denotes dual sensory loss. It would be another three years before I would need to register as totally blind. I had been divorced for five years when officially recognised as semi-sighted. I was no longer in denial about blindness and so preparations could be made for a future where I would live in the dark. When I was young I resolutely invested my identity in a career in the mainstream, marriage and children. These gave me meaning. Now I could clearly see that my place in the world was changing. I was divorced and I knew retirement was not far away. What would the future hold when I was totally blind?

The logical next step I told myself was to join a social club for the sight impaired but I discovered none existed. After a conversation with Social Services I created a group called Social Eyes. This was my first venture into socialising with blind people and I quickly realised this was not going to be easy and it became a one-man endeavour. Many people I came to know at that time used Braille. I still had some vestige of tunnel vision and was able to use a computer. Writing documents and building spreadsheets with limited sight is a tediously slow business but necessary for organising activities such as walks, talks and social evenings – and as usual I threw myself into the work.

A partially-sighted woman attended one of the events. Her name was Chrissie and she lived in Wokingham with a teenage daughter but was unhappily married and thinking of divorce. I also discovered that she suffered her own life-long disabilities. There was an immediate attraction and, despite our ailments, we began to sail together competing against able-bodied crews and enjoying country walks. We married two years later in 2000 and honeymooned at the Windermere Manor Hotel which is owned by the Guide Dogs Association. I learned to play blind chess here and it became our favourite place. It was the place I returned to after her death.

There is both joy and pain in any new relationship but a second marriage is accompanied by shadows from the past and although we had the shared experience of living with disability there would be times when we clashed. We could not force each other to become more convenient people but we could change for the better by implementing some sort of strategy out of mutual love and respect. Change often requires help from an intermediary in the form of another person or organisation. This facilitates a new perspective enabling individuals to see those negative aspects of character they would rather not acknowledge and help the stubborn minded to understand the challenges. I was well aware how tough this might be and could have refused to participate but where would this road have led? People can become indifferent to their circumstances ultimately acquiescing in hollowing half-lives that collapse without warning. It happened to my mother and father and I did not want to repeat those mistakes.

Chrissie was tough and refused to walk on eggshells. This was her strong point but I would discover many years later that this toughness had hurt my daughters. She would often tell me I was like my mother and with time I began to recognise personal attributes that made me unhappy. I grudgingly acknowledged my stubbornness, pride and independence. I had always thought I needed these characteristics to survive but now they were a relationship hindrance. They always had been there but dual sensory loss made me psychologically blind. I didn't like Chrissie's confrontations. They made me angry but with hindsight I could see they were nudging me towards some kind of personal honesty. I wanted to change but it was an emotionally exhausting process for both of us.

Despite these drawbacks we had a good relationship and in order to protect it I began to go to Greyfriars Church in Reading which marked the beginning of my journey into faith. We were willing participants in a marriage enrichment course but this quickly revealed unresolved episodes from my past. I was unwilling to admit to them at first but the more time I spent with Chrissie the more I saw someone who was very different to me and I persisted with the course which required painful engagement during the early stages. I was reluctant to understand the causes of our disagreements but I knew I should persevere until ultimately I sensed a hard rock lodged at my core. The more I tried to ignore it the more persistent it became until I saw it as self-centeredness and the cause of our arguments.

During these years Chrissie was blessed with comparatively good health and we enjoyed the same outdoor pursuits. We used the time constructively to work through the painful process of improvement. It enabled me to look inwardly and identify unpleasant truths that lurked beneath the superficial niceties. There came a point where I wanted to stop but there was no turning back with Chrissie. She would speak pointedly and I knew that together we were developing a more mature and robust relationship. It was necessary to go beyond the superficialities and take ownership of the failings; to go down in order to come up again. We were, in effect, managing change as management consultants might label the process – but we are not an organisation: we are flesh and blood.

This journey into self-awareness brought me to the edge of a deeper Christian faith. I recognised that the knowledge and willingness to learn from it were helpful and that only through self-examination and honesty could we hope to change. I wanted to become a more considerate partner for Chrissie but stubbornness is written into my DNA. I finally arrived at a place where I could listen to myself as well as others. Moderate-to-severe deafness has enhanced my ability to listen. I can quickly assess a person through their tone of voice, speed of speech, the content of their conversation and intonations in the voice. This ability was demonstrated when I received a summons for Jury service. At first I thought the Crown Prosecution Service had made a mistake and they would realise this when they met me. I returned the form certain that I would be excused this duty. Some days later I received a letter confirming my selection. I thought they had obviously not read my form properly and I was looking forward to surprising people at Reading Crown Court. On the first day of the trial I was met by a disability liaison officer and given a familiarisation tour of the courts and facilities and afterwards asked to explain what I remembered about the tour. Much to my surprise they announced that I had passed the test.

'But I can't see' I said.

He replied 'Oh that makes you a perfect juror because you are unable to judge people solely by appearances. Therefore you have to listen* and discern the truth of the matter'. The trial was about a minor burglary and assault on a police officer. After the closing speeches from the prosecutor and defence lawyers and the summing up by the judge we were shown into a private room to reach a verdict. Ten jurors found the defendant innocent but two of us thought him guilty.

'How can you know he's guilty?' asked a juror.

'Because he is lying'. I said.

Everyone had missed his contradictions but I had remembered every word.

As our relationship deepened I saw my behaviour mirrored by Chrissie's reactions. If she was my teacher it was because I recognised in her an enduring Christian faith that stayed with her even in the toughest times and this made it honest. I remembered how, unlike my brothers, I had frequently clashed with my mother. The emotional baggage some of us carry. I could not forgive my mother's biased stories that spawned my teenage resentment of my father. Thirty five years after that Friday when we agreed to the statement that 'he hasn't returned home' I visited him and learned a more rounded story and I felt she had robbed me of the years I could have enjoyed with him. My mother saw my visits as a betrayal. I realised that it was not my fault nor hers but the consequence of her circumstances. Chrissie had also suffered as a child but she had found a way to forgive.

When I was finally able to forgive my mother there was a sense of relief. I felt a sense of peace that I cannot exaggerate; the most beautiful moment in my life.

My love for Chrissie deepened as her agency changed me. She helped me escape a self-made prison; my upbringing, my mother's relentless fulmination against self-pity, and the subsequent determination to succeed in the hearing world. But this prison was of my own making. I alone had decided to bluff my way in the mainstream where I am disadvantaged. All this had made me hard and uncompromising. If only I had stopped to realise it was all so unnecessary. Gradually I found the promise of peace as I learned about 'grace'. This was the key and it broke the cycle of behaviour that wore me down. The means of escape arrived just in time as my life was about to take an unexpected and tragic turn.

*There is a hearing loop in court

19

The Grasshopper

Deep within the Columbian rainforest where Anthony and Sarah will one day walk a tiny grasshopper sits on a fern. Its antennae alive to the slightest stimuli transmitted through its world. Close by a lizard watches motionless. Two sacred life forms frozen in a life affirming ritual. The lizard strikes and destiny is fulfilled.

Chrissie Lawton had never been a well woman. From the age of two she had suffered Type 1 Diabetes that relentlessly attacked her organs and would eventually damage her sight. She fought against the limitations of diabetes however to live an active life, married and had a daughter. In the 1990s her kidneys began to fail and she was offered a kidney transplant in 1994. She met Anthony in 1996 when trapped in a marriage that had long been loveless and Anthony had been living in a desert for five years since his divorce in 1989. Each saw in the other someone who refused to be defined or subdued by physical disability and this is how their combined life began. He remembered wanting to invite Chrissie to his fiftieth birthday celebrations but decided against it because they had only recently met and she was by now in the process of divorcing. After a second kidney transplant the couple married in 2000. The new kidneys give

Chrissie strength and the couple are able to resume competitive dinghy sailing.

In 2003 Chrissie's health started to deteriorate again and the sailing had to stop. By late 2004 she was back on dialysis at the Royal Berkshire Hospital which kept her alive as Anthony became her carer for the next three years. During this period, around 2006, the couple agreed that Anthony should have a break and he discovered the Jubilee Sailing Trust. He signed up for a one week holiday of island hopping around the Canaries on a tall ship named after Lord Nelson. The adventure was successful and so in 2007 he signed up for a further three week passage to help sail the ship back to the UK from Madeira. This journey was too arduous however and he vowed never to sign up for such a long voyage again.

In 2007 everyone seems to be prospering not aware that the guardians of prosperity are too comfortable, deluded or nefarious. From their splendid towers the future looks unfaultable. No one notices cracks appearing in the foundation stones that support the world's financial systems. One of the most spectacular financial crashes in history follows a year later. It will be more devastating than the collapse of the South Sea Bubble or the Wall Street Crash. Lethargy or something more sinister affects the firmament and huge debts are built on subterfuge and opaque mechanisms. No one looks too closely as safety wires securing the edifice are cut relaxing regulations and so increasing trust in dubious products. The guardians sleep and disaster arrives.

Failures occur for all sorts of reasons. Chrissie had valued the life her transplant had given her in 2000 and the couple took full advantage enjoying outdoor adventures. Yet despite living responsibly Chrissie's new kidneys and Anthony's eyes were slowly deteriorating. Ultimately they led a precarious existence of a blind-deaf man pushing a semi-sighted woman in a wheelchair as she shouted frantic instructions. But they remained happy together as they put their wellbeing in each other's hands.

In 2007, when the world was falling apart, Chrissie is offered a double transplant of her pancreas and kidneys and does not hesitate. It is a pioneering procedure. The operation is successful and the replacement pancreas brings an end to her Type 1 Diabetes. For the first time since the age of two she is free from a daily blood testing regime and the uncertainty of a hypoglycaemic spike. But she does not acquiesce in this improved quality of life and despite new freedoms refuses to eat chocolate, drink alcohol or relax her strict diet. Alas even well managed investments carry risk. There are no perfect solutions in this life and a new threat emerges from the necessary use of anti-rejection drugs that enable her body to accept new organs.

These drugs suppress the immune system and in so doing introduce the secondary risk of cancer and just two years later in 2009 she is diagnosed with lymphoma. Chrissie is aware of the risks and bravely faces chemotherapy at the Royal Berkshire Hospital where she fights the returning cancer until only one desperate option is available to her; bone marrow transplantation. The process involves taking healthy stem cells from her body and harvesting them prior to chemotherapy or radiation treatment. It is a ruthless process that sterilises the blood which is temporarily stored while extreme chemotherapy is used to kill the remaining blood cells in her body. When the process is complete cleaned blood is returned. There is a high risk of death and the treatment is only offered as a last resort.

This extreme procedure has to be endured at a time when the anti-rejection drugs keeping her kidneys alive are weakening her immune system. She is facing overwhelming odds. The patient going into treatment does not have a healthy body; she is disadvantaged. The anti-rejection drugs do not encourage growth of new blood in the bone marrow. Chrissie and Anthony are aware that it is rare for someone who has suffered diabetes to survive chemotherapy and Anthony witnesses her decline. Both know there is only a small chance of success but despite her weakened state she proves again her ability to survive.

The battle against cancer is waged over three weary years and involves long stays in hospital. During these years Anthony is a carer rather than a husband and accompanies her everywhere. The journey begins at the Churchill Hospital in Oxford and with the help of relatives and friends he is able to visit her every day. She is eventually allowed home to recover under the care of the Royal Berkshire Hospital. After enduring three months of bone marrow treatment however her health begins to fail. She becomes very ill on Christmas Eve 2011 and is semi-conscious on Christmas Day. By evening she is clearly much worse and by midnight he phones the GP and arranges admittance to hospital where she lingers for a further two weeks.

Chrissie died in January 2012. Anthony recalls that she never complained and found his own inspiration in her resilience:

'I think her faith helped because she said God was always with her. She persevered. Even during treatment she remained stoical. Often in the past I would offer to take over some chore or task to give her rest but she would refuse and carry on. She was a fighter. We both had medical issues but both got on with life. We were well matched in this sense. Eventually even Chrissie was unable to resist the onslaught of bacteria, fungus and whatever else prospers in the absence of a healthy immune system. The irony was the cancer was cured. It was subsequent microbial inflection that killed her. She was an amazing woman'.

20

Surviving Chrissie

Chrissie's ability to laugh at hardship stayed with Anthony like the smile of Lewis Carroll's Cheshire cat, sometimes provocative but mostly amusing. 'We had the same ideas – always seeing some sort of black humour in our misadventures. Chrissie helped me realise that this is so important because life is tough. You must learn to laugh.'

Behind the humour was a steely faith that enabled the most daunting obstacle to be faced with resolve. Whatever the journey there had to be fun in the travelling and her humour was well-honed by a life time of challenges. Even during bone marrow transplants Chrissie's ability to smile won the respect of the medical team treating her. When the process was complete the consultant entered the recovery room and said compassionately 'Well done Chrissie you survived'.

Anthony also suffered pain during the last years; the psychological pain of a carer. 'I struggled because events were totally out of my control. I could only hold her hand. Carers always take the full brunt. All I could do was to be with her which seemed inadequate and this is immensely draining. I needed to remain strong and to absorb the relentless distress of her suffering. This was my role and duty as I sat beside her every day at the Churchill and Royal Berkshire Hospitals and later at home. She needed my support and this was going to be my life until she recovered or succumbed'.

He thought he was mentally prepared for the possibility of her death but despite his preparation he went into shock. The intense three year battle for survival fuelled by hope did not prepare him for the legacy of her going. The loss was almost too much to bear.

'Absence was a physical experience. Death is too abstract a term to explain what I was feeling at this time. My children had their own frenetic lives and I did not want to develop a dependency on them. Kirsty, my younger daughter was in Brighton and although immersed in studies to become a doctor visited me frequently. Sarah's career was in Sydney. It is not possible to be further from Reading other than leaving the planet. I knew I needed to take control of my emotional trauma but I did not know how. This was another challenge I needed to overcome but it was different now. I reminded myself that I had lived the best years building a career, raising a family, coping with setbacks and finding new solutions. I know I have to move on from this place. Sometimes you don't want to move on. Moving on too soon devalues what it is you are missing. The pain is a teaching space for those wishing to learn. There is no formal qualification for this learning just a deepening ability to empathise and accept that this is life and we accept what confronts us without superficial questions. Bereavement has to be embraced. The current time is always the best time because this is the time I am alive even if I don't like my immediate existence.

Age changes the priorities. The priority in the autumn years is to remain meaningful but the loss of Chrissie ripped away the desire to make adjustments or start anew. Life was going on around me but it was as if time had stopped and there was nothing apart from a visceral sense of being alone. Friends and family gathered around after her death and although I was not alone I felt alone and in a place that no one else could enter. By comparison when I became totally blind some years beforehand I felt a sense of relief because I no longer needed to make constant adjustments as my sight receded. When I became totally blind I realised that whatever I learned now would serve me the rest of my life. I had that certainty. But when Chrissie died there was no such succour in knowing the battle was over. There was no relief in that certainty.

I wanted to remember Chrissie's face but my memory was blank and my inability to look at a photograph added to my distress and sense of helplessness. Images provide a stimulus for the memory, nourish the emotions and soothe the orphaned heart. They help the bereaved to think beyond the picture and eulogise the past. But I did not have these emollient images to soften my angst and help subdue the recriminations of hindsight that tried to trick me into thinking I could have done better. Peace only comes through reconciliation with the imperfect self and the determination to do things better from this moment on. This is the true repentance and is more forgiving than a sentimental one. If I had been born blind photographs of Chrissie would not have been an issue because I would never have seen her. But there was a time, five years earlier, when I could see her. I may have lacked a wide field of vision but she featured sharply at the centre. I wanted to see her again – even if only a photograph. Now in my sorrow and distress I could not recall her image. Her face was a blank and this loss of image only made the loss greater.

My life became a visual blank from the moment my sight

completely failed. I lacked visual memories. Sleep and relaxation escaped me. I was a ghost of myself without sense of past or future. Just a relentless present moment and irreparable emptiness. This pain went deeper than I had expected. A cocktail of affliction replaced the anxiety and fear of isolation that had plagued my earlier life like a shadow. The shadow always knew my trepidation but now that it was upon me there was no longer a need to fear it. You can only fear the future because of what might happen. My present was a passive immersion in pain. Emotional pain is worse than physical pain. This unholy trinity of death, separation and loss so dominated me that fear no longer had a role – for now anyway. There would come a time when fear would return but now I needed to escape this pit of grief or it would destroy me. Every morning I woke to embrace an empty day and realised there was only me. Much of my life until now had been about hiding from myself. I relied on independence and pride to protect me from rejection whether from the deaf, the hearing or even the blind world. I thought I had prepared myself for this moment but the event showed I was not a rock. More than ever I realised I am a conscious interdependent person but the core motivator of that interconnection, the person I loved deeply, was gone.

When you are loved the loss of love cannot be over exaggerated. It is futile to fight it and you can't give in to it. You're not fit to be with others and you can't afford to be alone with yourself. But you have to come to terms with the new situation. You have to think about navigating the new landscape. I had yet to realise that the experience of bereavement is itself the cure. It cannot be instantly cured nor should it because psychological pain is rooted so deeply in the self. It must be endured until some form of post traumatic growth or whatever you want to call it begins to emerge. This is the doorway out of the prison and a starting point for the bereaved mind. Chrissie's life had had meaning and realising that meaning would become my road to recovery.

One year after her death I was becoming deeply unhappy with myself. This was before I had a guide dog and relied on a long red-and-white cane. The cane is a useful aid but in my current state I was unable to concentrate and repeatedly suffered injury with every bruising encounter denting my spirit. I would try to escape my emotional pain by visiting Reading's busy town centre where I would be aware of people around me but their busyness somehow emphasised my aloneness. I had always feared this condition. This is the fear that drove me into foolish and isolating self-reliance in my younger years. Living with loss and not knowing what to do about it is normal grieving and while some try to escape the agony of grief by immersing themselves in constant activity I tried to talk openly about my suffering. The catharsis of conversation however was minimal and through the following twelve months my resolution would crumble into the sea.

It was Chrissie's dying wish that I would hold on to my fledgling faith but I told her I didn't think I could without her. She was always the one that kept the fire burning, providing the fuel. She understood what I needed to hear and she told me in plain English. This is why her death was so painful. The loss was so great six months later I submitted to adult baptism at Greyfriars Church in Reading. What were my motives? Was it the true faith of the convert or the desire to honour her memory? This is what she longed to see but I was never ready. She never tried to manipulate me and would only ever speak of her faith when I raised a question. We were on a journey. When she died I thought what faith I had would fade but it became stronger. The agony of grief drove me deeper into my soul and praying for answers, asking why so much pain, and then I had what I can only describe as a spiritual episode. Was this wishful thinking or a genuine vision? I don't think we are given simple answers. We have a choice and are motivated one way or the other.

The secret to sanity according to 17th century scholar, Rev. Robert Burton, is to avoid becoming 'idle and solitary'. I knew I needed to get away but it was only when I began to feel completely lost that I remembered the Jubilee Sailing Trust. I had sailed with this charity five or six years previously. The second voyage had been too much for me but although I knew the proposed India-to-Australia voyage would be well beyond my comfort zone I signed up for the three-month passage. This was madness but I needed to push myself to the limit. The first voyage was from India to Singapore and the second would take me on to Perth, Australia. From there I would fly to Sydney to meet Sarah who was working with a firm of accountants. I hoped these arduous voyages would mollify the pain of grieving but the second voyage was to introduce a layer of suffering I had not anticipated'.

The *Lord Nelson* at sea © JST Tallshipstock

21

Black Sea. Bright Sky

John Shaw boarded the troop ship in Glasgow. In the darkness of night, on the 10th May 1943 it slipped out of port and headed for a secret destination. The ship was escorted into the North Atlantic by two Royal Navy destroyers that were then diverted for mine sweeping operations leaving the troop carrier alone and vulnerable. The ship continued its voyage knowing that German U-boats lurked beneath the black, anonymous waters of the Atlantic waiting in anticipation for a serendipitous meeting. Alan Turing, working in Hut 8 at Bletchley Park, had cracked the Enigma code decrypting secret German naval communications in July 1942 and it is possible that the locations of all U-boats operating in the Atlantic were known but could not be shared for reasons of national security. The troops waiting apprehensively for deliverance on board SS Argentina *wore their life jackets throughout the voyage, afraid to remove them.*

Had SS Argentina *perished with all hands the possibility of two faulty genes combining to afflict a future human would have been prevented and Anthony would not exist. But there is more to life than mere existence and disability will shape its own story. Anthony read about this moment of peril from a letter written decades later recalling John Shaw's war time adventures. He does not think of it today when the Jubilee Sailing Trust's tall ship* Lord Nelson *departs from the naval port of Kochi in Kerala on India's tropical Malabar Coast.*

The ship is bound for Galle on the southern tip of Sri Lanka en route to Singapore arriving 25 May. There are around 40 crew members half of whom are disabled.

Kerala has an exposed shoreline of 600 km along which pirates cruise unseen waiting to greet unsuspecting vessels. It can be a lucrative business and anyone is fair game. The territorial waters of the subcontinent were dangerous places to sail in 2013. In December The Times of India *ran the headline 'Indian Waters third worst for pirate attacks'. It explained that after many trouble-free years a new series of incidents heralded the return of the marauders'.*

As if echoing a distant memory of family history the tall ship was escorted into international waters by two naval destroyers. The Lord Nelson *was then left to continue its voyage alone. According to reports land-based organised criminals assisted the pirates operating throughout the Singapore Strait and Strait of Malacca and far beyond into the South China Seas. The tall ship would transit these hostile waters as it headed out on a two-leg voyage to Freemantle, Australia via Singapore, Bali and the Cocos Islands.*

Anthony flew from Heathrow with a Jubilee Sailing Trust (JST) member of the ship's crew, Roger. They had met briefly before the voyage. Nigel another crew member who would impact Anthony's life flew separately to Bombay and then took a flight down to the port of Kochi in the southern state of Kerala where he joined the *Lord Nelson*. On seeing the three masted square-rigged sailing barque in the dockyard, he thought how sleek she appeared. A JST official introduced himself and immediately 'buddied' him with Anthony who was described as both deaf and blind and this led to an enduring friendship as Nigel recalls:

'There were others who were seeking adventure or to escape the circumstances of their lives or perhaps discover themselves.

If so, this was going to be facilitated through hard work, monotonous routines and the discipline required to control a large ship sailing the high seas around the clock. I knew Anthony's reasons for signing on and we quickly became friends. I was impressed that the loss of hearing and sight did not deter him from tackling almost any task on board apart from climbing the rigging which he was only allowed to do when the ship was tied up in dock. I respected Anthony's fearlessness and as time went by I thought him more able than some of the able-bodied crew'.

The voyage was to take them from Kochi on 28 April 2013 to Singapore arriving 25 May. The professional crew included mates and second mates, a purser and engineers to ensure the *Lord Nelson* operated as a proper merchant navy ship. The paying crew were formed into four watches. The average age of the non-professional crew was sixty four, the oldest was eighty four and Anthony was sixty six. Amongst the disabled crew, three were totally blind, two were wheelchair users, some were war wounded and there were many others with non-specific disabilities. The crew slept in bunks in dedicated male and female cabin dormitories. Those who were 'buddied' were allocated two bunk cabins, curtained off to provide some privacy. Anthony and Nigel were given the last available two berths on the women's side and Anthony was allowed to use their toilets and showers. This was much to their annoyance according to Nigel because he kept leaving items of clothing around requiring Nigel to collect the discarded items to keep the peace. To avoid any further embarrassment Nigel added extra rigging such as rope handles to stop Anthony walking into the women's bunks.

The ship's departure was delayed by three days due to issues with passports and visas allowing the crew time to explore Kochi which is both a tourist destination and an Indian naval base. Before leaving they were also invited to attend an official reception at the Indian Navy Club. Nigel's chief concern was that he had never looked after a blind person before and had to learn how to walk with predictable movements and instructions with Anthony walking behind him with his hand on his shoulder. This enabled him to tell from Nigel's body movements whether he was going right or left or up or down.

'It was a big advantage to share a bunk with a deaf person because I could make as much noise as I liked once Anthony had switched off his hearing aid. It would have taken an earthquake to awaken him. I quickly realised Anthony liked to be self-reliant. After he was shown where his locker was I left him to organise it unaided and apart from the occasional discarded item in the shower area Anthony kept everything in the right order. Most of the time he could find what he wanted when he needed it.

So, on the 1st May we sailed out of Kochi harbour under power for the first destination, Galle, on the southern tip of Sri Lanka. There was an air of excitement and expectation but after twenty minutes the engine was shut down. The problem was caused by refuse in the water. Floating rubbish had been sucked into the ship's water intakes. The first leg had lasted less than half an hour before the ship needed to drop anchor to allow the filters to be cleared. The unpleasant task was undertaken by an Indian Naval Officer we had met at the reception the previous evening. He was the first Indian to sail solo around the world and had accompanied us out of the harbour on his yacht to say goodbye. He happened to have rudimentary diving equipment on board and was able to go down and clear the intakes.

I noticed how quickly Anthony adjusted to life on board.

This was due in part to his lifelong experience as a dinghy sailor and to a previous experience of sailing a Tall Ship. He knew how they worked and only occasionally did I need to help him with directions on deck. There is a lag in the steering system of a large vessel so that when the ship's wheel is turned the boat will not respond immediately. This requires a judged response otherwise the boat will zig zag as the helm constantly corrects the direction trying to stay on course. Anthony knew how to do this and steered the ship economically. An audio system is used to announce the compass bearing and relevant instructions. Anthony was able to hear it although even with a top quality digital hearing aid he needed to put his head close to the loud speaker when steering in heavy winds. Crew members are required to work with the rigging whether limbless or able bodied and Anthony excelled at rope work. Everyone is given a rota of chores including cleaning the heads (toilets), scrubbing decks, varnishing, painting and cooking when not helming.

We arrived at our first destination, Galle, on the southern tip of Sri Lanka, after a three-day sail. The ship was secured to the harbour wall and Anthony's eager wish to climb the main mast was fulfilled. As his 'buddy' I needed to accompany him and we were attached to life lines. This is how sails are raised and lowered at sea by able-bodied crew who climb the mast and then traverse the mast spars or yards. When Anthony reached the top of the tallest mast he patted it and began to descend without a hint of uncertainty.

Whenever Anthony walked along city streets of Galle with his cane he drew a lot of attention as he done previously in India. The blind do not tend to venture out and so Anthony's independence attracted their curiosity. They wanted to know what he was doing on such a ship and why? We visited a tea plantation and tasted spices and peppers and cinnamon bark. A taxi driver was fascinated with Anthony and took us to sample some authentic Sri Lankan food.

Departure from Galle coincided with warnings of a cyclone in the Bay of Bengal. With so many disabled people on board safety netting needed to be rigged around the ship to reduce the risk of anyone being washed overboard. The captain decided to change course and sail south to cross the equator which is a cyclone free zone and thereby avoid the roughest seas and then turn north east to head for the top of Malaysia and from there sail down the Straits of Malacca. There is limited opportunity for entertainment under sail as the crew are in a rota of two and four hour watches and in the morning everyone helps with cleaning duties. Crossing the equator did provide one such opportunity. Anyone doing this for the first time is encouraged to participate in a Pollywog ceremony which is an excuse for silliness. Anthony entered into the ceremony whole heartedly and emerged in the time honoured way as a 'Black Shell'. Our next destination was Langkawi Island off the North West coast of Malaysia. The island is renowned for its natural beauty where powder-fine sandy beaches slip into a turquoise sea beneath swaying coconut trees. Virgin rain forest and rolling rice fields secrete cascading waterfalls and picturesque fishing villages. This is not quite the isolated paradise it sounds as the commercial development of shopping and entertainment centres have long since turned the tropical wilderness into a tourist hub.

The *Lord Nelson* was moored for two days in the Royal Langkawi Yacht Club and when a group of us decided to explore the area we asked Anthony for his preference. Bizarrely, he said "underwater world". This is a large aquatic visitor centre. No one could understand what Anthony would get out of this since he is blind but they failed to realise his more acute senses enable him to enjoy most types of visits especially when shared with others. The group travelled in a cable car and noticed how the experience of being suspended in the air captivated him. They described to him waterfalls swollen by the monsoon in the north and Anthony wanted to walk up one of them. We did this allowing him to make an accompanied climb to the top and down again although with hindsight this had been a dangerous – even foolhardy venture.

Anthony then did something far more courageous; swimming in the sea. He had a tendency to become disorientated and swim out to sea and I had to shout frequent instructions to turn 90 degrees and swim parallel to the beach. 'It struck me then, and I had been with him a long time by now, that this was a very brave thing to do. More brave than climbing up the mast'. Anthony had to trust that I would not lose sight of him.

The incident that touched me most deeply however was at three in the morning when we were on watch duty. The ship was heading south and tacking through the edge of the cyclone. A big storm broke and the sky was filled with lightning and thunder. One particularly large flash illuminated the ship and its sails and caused Anthony to jump from shock.

'What was that'?

'A lightning strike' I said.

'I saw it' he said excitedly 'I saw it''.

It was a wonderful moment for Anthony. It showed that the nerves in his eyes were still vaguely operating but not strongly enough for him to see. It was a moment that contributed to my deeper appreciation of Anthony's companionship. I realised that being buddied with a blind-deaf man did not rob me of any part of an adventurous holiday but added to the richness of discovery, partly experienced through the mind of a blind man. The responsibility for Anthony's safety helped me see the world we were traversing through different eyes. It was so enjoyable sharing experiences with someone who managed to squeeze so much out of every moment. He was never miserable or showed any signs of bitterness. By the end of the trip everyone knew and liked Anthony, he was popular. I came to understand that the purpose of his voyage was to escape grief following the death of Chrissie but he never succumbed to self-pity. During our harbour watches Anthony and I spent a lot of time talking about his late wife and how events in our lives had unfolded.

Lord Nelson reached Singapore, on 22 May after 2,503 nautical miles of sailing totalling 16 days, 8 hours and 26 minutes at sea. During this time a friendship group formed around Anthony. The ship was given special permission by the harbour authorities to moor beside the Vivo Shopping Mall where the crew could walk off the gang plank and into the smartest shops on the island. They were treated to a special meal by the Norton Rose accountancy firm who were sponsors of the JST Round-The-World voyage. Nigel and Anthony visited the Sands Rooftop Skyline, 57 floors up with an infinity pool and gardens and subsequently the Bay Zoological Garden. This held particular appeal to Anthony due to the many thousands of plant species with their various textures and wide ranging fragrances. Singapore, with its generous provision for disabled access, made it easy for Anthony to explore the city. Nigel reminisced:

'I will always remember Anthony standing on the specially

adapted bow sprit with the wind blowing sea spray in his face. It is a delightful experience even for people who can't see. Life on board can become monotonous at times and to see Anthony going up the bow sprit was uplifting. He couldn't see or hear but he could feel the salt spray on his face and sense the changing movements of the ship and its speed when the sails were being trimmed. It brings alive other sensory perceptions. I was grateful to Anthony. The trip was inspirational. Would I do it again? I am not sure I would get as much enjoyment without someone like Anthony to share the challenges. It was uplifting to be with some-one recovering their enthusiasm for life. It made me feel quite humble. He and I enjoyed life together for that short while and it was such an experience that I took my wife and grandchildren to meet him the following year when he was on a canal boat in Wiltshire near our family home'.

1. JST tall ships draw people from every type of background and national-ity; Americans, Kosovans, New Zealanders, Irish, South Africans, Hong Kong Chinese *et al*.

2. Severely disabled people are accommodated in eight wheelchair cabins while everyone else sleeps in dormitory-style quarters. The ship's equipment includes power-assisted steering for the ship's wheel, a speaking compass and visual and tactile alarms to support emergency announcements. Sig-nage and diagrams in Braille to help the blind find their way around the ship which included accessible toilets, large lifts and wider passageways for wheelchair access.

22

Log from the Java Sea and Indian Ocean

'It is always worth double checking the small print. Some months before embarking on the two-leg voyage from India to Australia, I discovered a distressing oversight: on arrival in Singapore the *Lord Nelson* would be used for a private charter. I was the only member of crew to have signed up for the two legs and would be alone in an unfamiliar city for two weeks. This is a daunting prospect for someone who is deaf and blind.

'JST told me it was too late to cancel the booking but that another crew member, Roger, was visiting China from Singapore and perhaps I could join him? This seemed like a big ask at first. Who would want to be lumped with a deaf-blind man when touring China? Anyway, I called him at home and he agreed to visit me in Reading with his wife. His enthusiasm delighted me. He thought nothing of accompanying a deaf-blind man. He organised the tickets and the tour and we shared the costs. I felt saved although it presented the challenge of flying back to Singapore alone and then spending a week in a strange city. It was during a conversation at church when explaining my dilemma to friends, that a stranger overhearing our conversation introduced himself and offered a remedy. Nigel was a semi-retired businessman who had spent most of his life in Malaysia. He offered to fly out and meet me at Singapore airport on my return from Beijing. The journey would enable him to catch up with old friends. This seemed like an answer to prayer. A week in China with Roger followed by a week in Singapore with Nigel would transform a two-week emotional abyss into a fortnight of shared activity. The human collider was clearly at work.

'I flew with Roger from Heathrow to Kochi and shared a taxi to the docks. I remember the heat was overwhelming. India was a frying pan. There was an hour's drive to Kochi naval base but it felt like two lifetimes. The taxi ride was not like taking a black cab from Paddington to St James. From the moment we set off, I was thrown around the back seat. The driver was frantically accelerating and braking, swerving and sounding the car horn and shouting at people as it lurched wildly from side to side. There was a cow resting in the middle of the road apparently. At this moment I would have preferred Alton Towers – at least they have safety certificates. In the midst of the chaos Roger spoke calmly into my hearing aid, "I'm glad you can't see what's going on Anthony". Roger remembered the incident:

'This was Anthony's welcome to India and he survived to tell the tale. We had arrived a day early and the locals were taking a close interest in this strange man walking with a white red-and-white cane as we explored the area. Potholes and rubbish littered the streets although there was no olfactory evidence of decay. I organised a visit to a fresh food restaurant so that Anthony could experience the flavours'.

If the first leg on *Lord Nelson* had been a personal success for Anthony the second leg could have been a disaster had it not been for two more companions, Robin Ready and a blind Australian, Craig. It was, according to Anthony, a voyage too far exacerbated by an injury, rough seas and a change of crew.

'The second leg from Singapore to Fremantle suffered wild weather. During the early days turbulent seas caused me to fall and injure my arm so that I was unable to raise it above my shoulder. This affected my proud sense of independence and limited what I was able to do on deck. Much of the time I was constrained below deck with the other disabled as we were sailing through gale force storms causing the ship to roll through 80 degrees. It was considered unsafe to be on deck for much of the time and I became resentful since I had sailed these ships before and survived in rough conditions. I always want to be amongst the action. The ships are equipped for disabled people but Health & Safety requirements and the worry of litigation in the event of an accident give charities like JST little choice. Disabled people are stowed away with the provisions. But I am an experienced sailor. I am alert, cautious and self-reliant. Stick me on the rigging please. As the storm tossed the ship in the Java Sea a storm of resentment raged in my mind but it was also during these long idle periods below deck that I was able to reflect on happier times such as the visit to China.

I had flown to Beijing with Roger and spent three days in the north of the country where we saw the Terracotta Army. I was allowed to touch replicas of the soldiers and imagined their shape and detail. Every figure was different. We went into one of the many large pits containing the figures and walked around the edge of the motionless gathering. The scale was overwhelming and for some reason I struggled to comprehend what was standing before me. It was like seeing the sea for the first time as a small child with no previous experience to help my mind comprehend the vast flat expanse or when as a teenager told I would go blind and imagined a vast dark and empty future before me.

How does a blind-deaf person extract any experience from a sight-seeing holiday? The secret lies in using the remaining senses. It helped that I remembered pictures of the Terracotta Army before going blind. Now they seemed like pyramids buried for thousands of years in the tomb of the first emperor of China, Qin Shi Huang. I couldn't see anything but I could imagine the craftsmen toiling to make these soldiers centuries earlier. What hardships did they endure? Their work connected us across the passage of time emphasising our insignificance. We flew back to Beijing and spent three or four days visiting Tiananmen Square Palace and the Forbidden City with an official guide.

'I recall the sense of history, scale and smells. The smells were pleasant. We visited markets and tried various foods with Roger describing the environment. I knew people were looking at us. The guide took us to a traditional Chinese community to meet the residents. It consisted of low buildings surrounded by a square courtyard with a tree in the centre. Eating out was a particular pleasure. Sometimes we slipped out unaccompanied into narrow side streets off the tourist map where we encountered new smells, canopies of laundry and various metal items clanging above our heads. We stepped into a shop where I could hear and visualise dozens of household items suspended from the ceiling. We must have been the only foreigners walking into these places. We were not tourists now but travellers and the experience revealed something of the life of ordinary Chinese people. This was real life and not some caricature of it served up on a plate for detached tourists. You might be surprised how much I see and hear'.

The two travellers moved on to visit the Great Wall of China where once again Anthony would experience a moment of euphoria. 'To say the wall is huge is both a statement of the obvious and an understatement. It is not simply long but unexpectedly wide and deep as I paced its width and experienced it through my haptic senses and kinaesthetic learning. I could feel the excitement of people around me. I walked up it, across it and along it until we reached an observation tower. There was a dark room at the top of the tower and I was taken to a tiny window that looked out onto mountainside lit by acute sunlight. On rare occasions certain light conditions affect my eyes enabling me to see blurred images. This was such a day and I saw a vague white line snaking through the dark background. Roger said the dark areas were forests but I could see this tiny thin line.

'Is that the wall?' I shouted

'Yes' he said.

'Wow' I exclaimed. I was seeing the wall winding its way over the hills to meet the horizon. When you are blind any moment like this is intensely emotional. I cried at seeing this weaving white line in the dark. This was a fitting end to our sojourn through China as our personal paths would now separate. Roger would head off for Heathrow and I would return to Singapore. I find travelling alone without the help of an able-bodied companion stressful even though I have airport assistance. On arrival in Singapore, an airport assistant put me in a wheel chair, which is normal procedure, but then instead of taking me through to the arrivals lounge to meet Nigel, delivered me to Customs for interrogation. This was not friendly.

'Why have you returned from China?'

'I am returning to join the *Lord Nelson*'.

'It is very unusual for someone like you to go from Singapore to China and then return here'.

The officials questioning me seemed insensitive and suspicious. Eventually I found the repeated questions and their refusal to accept my explanation exasperating. They obviously did not understand the term 'tall ship'.

'I'm re-joining the *Lord Nelson*. It's docked in Singapore. It's on television and in the newspapers. Haven't you read about it'? I said sternly.

They released me and I met Nigel as planned. Meeting up with him was a huge relief. He organised a hotel and, at last, I could relax. We visited a sky bar on top of Singapore's tallest building and I enjoyed the swimming pool where I became aware of peacocks wandering around and squawking. It was an exotic sound. Companionship had soothed my inner demons. I was not alone. At the end of the week we said our goodbyes. Nigel flew to Malaysia and I returned to the ship and met Craig, the visually impaired Australian who had travelled up to Singapore. He was the only other blind crew on this leg of the voyage. He introduced me to the benefits of using a smartphone adapted for the visually impaired. I was impressed with his proficiency and this gave me hope for the future. I had bought one before leaving the UK but only made calls. He showed me how to use the message app and Mail and introduced me to apps and the benefits of using a smartphone keyboard. He insisted that I should buy a keypad before the ship left harbour and I thought 'this device is going to change my life'.

Sunday 9 June 2013. The previous six-week leg to Singapore had left me feeling exhausted and I did not want to continue. At the outset of this voyage something happened that was an indication of what was to come. Within a matter of days I became aware of cliques. These are not healthy on a long voyage because the limited space can exaggerate feelings of isolation. I realised that that the clique is uncertain in knowing how to include a deaf-blind person. I like to be self-reliant but do not want to feel alone. I also recognise that conformity with the clique is not the healthy way forward as I would be endorsing it. As we headed out into the South China Sea I looked for an escape and I was grateful for Robin who became a congenial buddy. We took the first night watch. I was relieved to discover that Robin trusted me to complete tasks without having to be constantly monitored. A bond of friendship developed that would eventually lead to my joining future adventures on his yacht. The following day our course took us along the north coast of Sumatra and people described the beauty of double rainbows around the sun and clouds. We cross the equator and enter a more turbulent Java Sea with the coastline of Borneo on the port side. I began to feel the rejection of the cliques more acutely as they excluded me from their company during communal activities such as the so-called Happy Hour which is not the early evening drinking hour but the early morning duty of cleaning and maintaining the ship.

Sometimes I had to argue to be included in duties that were rightfully mine – such as participating at the helm because some members thought the ship could not be entrusted to someone with dual sensory loss. I remembered the story of a solo sailor: a man in his eighties, who had once served with SOS (precursors to the SAS) during World War II. He frequently performed well in races at his sailing club despite the frailty of his age. He had sailed the lake so many times he could predict wind patterns with his eyes closed. This was true for me now. My previous experience meant I knew the routines and I could feel the behaviour of the ship and the weather. I had, for example, a sensitivity to freshening winds whenever we approached weather fronts and the audible compass was sufficiently loud to enable me to stay on course.

We were well into the voyage when the time came for me to give a talk on Visual and Hearing Impediments. The presentation seemed to go well and I received positive feedback. Afterwards Robin and I took the midnight to 4am watch and Robin reported weather conditions in the Java Sea to the Greenwich main records centre.

Sunday 16 June 2013. There is a church service before the mast. Later I am told people reported seeing dolphins and flying fish during the morning sail-training session.

We arrive at Bali harbour at 9.45am on 18 June and wait for the harbour pilot to take us into the ship's berth at the southern end of the island. We have time to explore the resort before the evening meal. Next day we visit a World Heritage site that includes ancient temples and paddy fields. In the evening a group of children from a local orphanage perform a Hawaiian dance on the quayside and the crew donate generously to the charity. We leave Bali on the morning of June 20th and I feel exhausted due to weeks of disrupted sleep and changing night duty on the bridge. Some nights this is from 8pm to midnight, then midnight to 4am the following night and then my favourite shift, which is from 4am to 8am when I see the sunrise. This is the best time of day for me because although I have no useful vision I can see the light increase as the sun rises and this is an exciting experience. We make a grand exit under a full set of sails but it is not long before a freshening wind requires us to furl them and we plough through a rolling and lumpy sea. The rough conditions continue into Friday 21st but on Saturday conditions have lightened and the ship can motor-sail. The crew encounter a fishing fleet and trade a bottle of whisky and nine dollars for a number of barramundi fish from local fishermen. Everyone thinks it is a fair deal.

By Sunday 23rd weather conditions worsen. The sea is rough and the captain has to abandon a visit to Christmas Island due to heavy swells and a severe weather forecast. The weather becomes so wild it is considered unsafe to have disabled people on deck. Presentations and talks about navigation, celestial positioning and the purpose of rigging lighten my mood and allow time to improve my proficiency with the smartphone and keyboard. Robin and I take the 4am watch as we near the Cosus or Keeling Islands at 9.30am. These islands form a horseshoe shaped archipelago and the depth of the seabed changes almost instantly from thousands of fathoms to a few metres. It is quite startling. The Cosus Islands are a remote territory of Australia consisting of two coral atolls made up of 27 smaller islands lying a thousand nautical miles off the North West coast of Australia.

Saturday 29 June. I listen to the crew's excitement at seeing five-foot baby sharks and waves breaking over coral reefs.

Sunday 30 June. We have moored in the shallow waters of the horseshoe archipelago and have a day of freedom. We take a dingy to visit one of the islands that is thickly populated with invisible coconut trees silently swishing in the wind. I experience a strange crunching sensation as I walk with Robin along the beach. He describes the scenery and explains that we are walking over many thousands of small red crabs racing in all directions. Eventually we find a crab-free area and stop to swim in the warm water and enjoy lunch. This feels like paradise after so many hours at sea.

Alas, we leave paradise and sail into a strengthening 20-knot wind, described as a fresh breeze on the Beaufort Wind Scale and is sufficiently strong to create a big swell in the ocean. On Tuesday the wind increases from 20 to 25 knots and engine alarms are set off at 1.30am as one engine fails to start and some sails are raised. We are still just about sailing but now on the wrong course due to the wind. By Wednesday 3rd the wind has risen to 30 knots but thankfully both engines are now working.

On Thursday 4 July winds have increased to 35 to 40 knots and are described as moderate to gale force and the ocean swell is now four to five metres deep. People with disabilities are again confined below decks.

The ship pitches and rolls dramatically in heavy rain during the next 48 hours. Conditions have calmed by Sunday 7 July and the engines are again shut down as we make progress under a full set of sails in 10 to 15 knot winds. On Tuesday we change course 100°. I am permitted on deck in sunny light winds. The next day Robin and I are on night duty from midnight and people on deck talk of a sky full of stars. The skyscape sounds beautiful and is invisible. It is July 11th and we are now just 850 miles from Perth and I can enjoy the light winds. By Saturday 13th there is a large ocean swell and heavy rains. By Sunday 14th,we have covered 4,050 miles in predominately stormy conditions. Not far to go now and my spirits are up but on Tuesday 16th there are storm force winds and very high seas.

Day 41 of the leg and although confined again below decks as the ship is tossed around in stormy conditions I am pleased to hear that the *Lord Nelson* has recorded its fastest ever speed at 14.2 knots. The wind increases to 60 knots but this impedes our progress and our speed is reduced to 12.5 knots. By Wednesday

17 July the seas have calmed in a breezy 20 knot wind. Rotnest Island, which lies off the coastline of Perth, is sighted and by 9.30 pm we are moored in Fremantle. Australia at last. We have completed a voyage of 4,578 nautical miles and I am emotionally drained and happy the sea voyage is over. It has done its work. I feel I have come to terms with Chrissie's passing. The emotional trauma has subsided. I can now move on with my life. I have reached the end of a six-and-a-half-week passage across two major oceans. A kind of odyssey. I had promised myself I would not repeat a long voyage after sailing from the Canaries to Southampton many years previously. It just shows how the memory of trials is softened by the passage of time. All that remains before returning home are two coast-to-coast crossings of Australia; east to west and north to south.

Bring it on'.

23

Australia at Last

'Thursday 18th July. No more sailing. No more sailing. Hooray. The crew walk into Freemantle which is part of the metropolitan area of Perth and enjoy a dinner of steak, chips and real ale which Robin clearly enjoys. He tells me that his duties at the helm in stormy seas have exhausted him and at times he had struggled to remain standing. I am in a good frame of mind too because my injured arm is less painful. I had torn a ligament and muscle fibres while lifting a hatch cover just two days into the second voyage. I felt something snap and experienced a pain so sharp I almost fainted and was taken to the ship's doctor who recorded the incident. It meant having limited use of my arm for the rest of the journey. On Saturday 20 July there's a trip to an indoor market. I sense the buzz of the crew and the rich smells of fresh food coming from one of the port's famous markets. We visit a long disused hilltop prison that once processed British convicts destined for Perth. The following day is the last day and I travel to the airport. I am flying to Sydney to meet Sarah.

Airport regulations require me to be ferried around in a wheel chair from the point of arrival through to the gate and then onto the plane. This made flying around Australia relatively easy compared to what I would experience when travelling around

South America in 2016. At that future date I will arrive in Bogota airport to be met by Sarah and her partner James and explore the city with my long red-and-white cane. She will tell me it is one of the most dangerous cities in the world with drug cartels but that I shouldn't worry because there are a lot of police officers armed with machine guns on patrol. I will tell her 'I am relaxed' although the thought of a blind-deaf man and his daughter and partner caught up in the cross fire of a gun fight between drug dealers and police with automatic weapons will not console me. She will give me a running commentary as we cruise the streets of the capital telling me that people are looking at us because she is blond and I am blind. Once again various tactile experiences add to my joy of travel. Sarah will take time to describe the architectural styles of buildings and their materials. With my enhanced hearing aids I hear street noises ricocheting off them and it helps me understand their appearance which is heightened when I touch them. We will move on to an entirely different type of adventure and brush with mortality. It will begin with a trip to a coffee plantation and then a guided trek through the rainforest. Despite the basic farm accommodation the coffee tasting will fascinate me as I happily explore aromas, roasts and regions.

The trek into the rain forest will lead me along uneven muddy paths where I slide precariously and eventually need the help of two people to remain upright. The loss of Chrissie will have softened as I step through undergrowth that hinders my steps. A thick humidity and ominous silence permeates the forest. This is not a place to become lost or make mistakes. I concentrate and feel alive. The trek will seed good memories up to the point when Sarah is bitten by a large black and white bug. She is a tough and adventurous soul but this is a nasty bite and I know she is in pain. We will need professional medical help and we head back to the main hospital in Bogota with its specialist department for tropical diseases and bites. Sarah has very limited Spanish and we will become trapped in a five hour merry-go-round. I will worry that no one understands the problem until in the midst of this humid and crowded hospital a stranger overhears our panicked conversation and offers to help us find the right department where we find an English-speaking doctor.

Memories of the rainforest will remain with me; swimming in a hot pool fed by a sulphurous waterfall that is too hot for comfort and encountering the strange texture of rain-forest Wax trees. We will travel on to Peru only to be delayed at the airport by low cloud. The clouds disperse and I hope they do not return as we fly towards Lima over mountainous Peru and then on to Cusco where we will trek in the thin air some 3,500 metres above sea level. I will need to slow down. This is the Inca trail and we will walk up what feels like thousands of ancient uneven steps. Every step is different and without vision I will have to use my feet and long red-and-white cane to feel my way to the top. I will not want to hold everyone up but if I rush and fall I could be the cause of a much longer delay. In this future trek as the group snakes its way to the top I will wonder about those ancient captives forced to make this trip for the purposes of ceremonial slaughter. But this is all in the future.

I have arrived in Sydney and am meeting Sarah for the first time after many years. I am happy to take things easily having experienced a demanding voyage across two oceans and then flying to Sydney. I had been too ambitious but it is over now and the effort has achieved the purpose of changing my state of mind. I can relax and enjoy this precious time with my daughter before heading north to Brisbane.

The playground of Queensland unexpectedly gave me time to practice with the smartphone. I discover how to arrange and change schedules, hold conversations and explore various apps that meet specific needs as I enjoy this country-meets-town city. My confidence grows and I feel less isolated as I fly from Brisbane to Canberra to meet up with another friend. Time now seems to move more quickly as the tour draws to an end. I fly back to Sydney and then with Sarah to the UK to attend the wedding of my daughter Kirsty and her fiancé Tom in West Sussex. The final days in Sydney provide valuable space allowing me to compose and commit to memory my father-of-the-bride wedding speech. I have no ability to write or use braille. The only way I can prepare a speech is to think and memorise it – there will be no crib sheets to help me on the day.

And so the world tour ended somewhere in West Sussex when the weekend of the wedding arrived. Kirsty and I stayed in different hotels but I was able to visit her before the wedding service. It is one of my favourite recollections as I was able to touch the fabrics of the wedding dress and hairstyle and imagine her appearance.

She looked beautiful and this gave me great joy.

24

Implosion

You can't suppress things for ever. Like a ball held under water, memories and their associated emotions require effort to keep them hidden. It only takes a moment or unexpected comment to wrest the ball from your grasp.

'I don't remember quite how it happened, but I was with my ex-wife Rowena and suddenly through no fault of hers I became angry and rude and simply wanted to walk away. Later I would understand that my anger was related to loss and rejection, fear and grieving. I thought of myself as a rock but this was a weakness not an inner strength. I was proud of my refusal to ask for help. I was afraid to tell people about my failing sight and hid the truth behind my limited hearing. I tried to fool the world.

During the long years of subterfuge I did not realise how refusal to confide in others would simply make life harder. The grievances began in infanthood when I felt I had been abandoned in hospital, then sent to board at a Deaf and Dumb school, then my parents' divorce – especially when my mother prevented me from visiting my father and there was constant ridicule from school and work which persisted into early adulthood. I had never fully accepted my own divorce. I felt the children were being snatched away – even though Rowena and

I continued to attend school events together and I enjoyed holidays with them.

All my life I had been in search of relationships but denial and self-reliance limited the possibilities. Most people want to share something of themselves but I was afraid to reveal the truth about my hearing and my failing sight. I hid my feelings until the dam burst. Tears poured uncontrollably. They washed away the deep seated need to be in control. My independence was revealed as a façade. I would pull myself together only to break down again and this behaviour was to continue for a period of time. I succumbed to feelings of injustice. Deafness and blindness were unfair. Divorce and Chrissie's death cruel. I remembered how the other parents were able to help my daughter and son-in-law with their car. I wanted to help because of my own expertise with cars but it was not possible. Nor could I help much with the grandchildren. My granddaughter Emelina is three and takes my hand and leads me to the dining table because, she says, I have 'broken eyes'. I'm deaf and blind and she wants to help me. She understands that toys can be broken. Seventeen years had passed since my divorce and four since the death of Chrissie and although I dealt with bereavement on the Indian Ocean these other losses revisited me with vengeance. How does anyone know they have built a harmful identify until everything starts to unravel? I have taken many forms of risks but refused to risk being open about disability. I was angry. I turned my back on everything – even prayer.

An incident stayed with me from my youth. As a young person I want to meet girls and the obvious place to socialise is the night club. Here is a problem. These noisy, frenetic places are not the friendliest environments for someone with faulty ears and eyes. The subdued lighting, flashing lights and loud pulsating music and DJs is a confusing mélange assaulting my senses. Everybody shouts. Unfortunately the raised volume does not help as everything is equally loud. They are difficult places for me to navigate as the interiors seem to drip liquid reflections from lacquered panels and polished metal trim. Light bursts explosively in my eyes. I alternate between darkness and dazzle but this is where the young women congregate and I am desperate to meet them despite the hazards. The disco of this era is the very definition of cool except I struggle and this is the last place anyone wants to look clumsy.

I would never have risked ballroom dancing. Here I am free to step alone onto the dance floor amongst gyrating bodies where there is little risk of stepping on a partner's feet.

One Saturday night I overcome my reticence and step out of the margins and to my horror find myself facing a girl in the flashlight void. I ask if she would like to dance. I chance an opening remark which is probably clumsy or inept but I hope to attract a positive response. The music is so loud I have no chance of holding a conversation. I have been told that if you want to attract girls you need to listen to them and not talk about yourself. Listen intently. The night club is not the most sensible location for starting a conversation with anyone. This is difficult for me even in normal circumstances. The flashing lights and noise flood my mind with existential questions. I feel self-conscious and in the flashes of light I occasionally perceive a pair of eyes looking at me. Then confusion. In the kaleidoscope I see flaying arms and legs and am disorientated. I have no idea where I am on the dance floor or what happened to my newly found dance partner. And now she is gone. It is as I feared, the loud music and flashing lights mean I can neither see nor hear her and before long I am lost in the crowd. I imagine her embarrassment at my presumed callous and bizarre behaviour. At this moment my identity is that of a lemon.

At this moment on the dance floor, reduced to feeling foolish and alone, I realise my mistake. I should have explained my sensory loss beforehand and she might have kept in step with me but such honesty would invite rejection – or so I thought'.

The deepest part of any relationship is communication. Anthony's real fear was that without a career and some trappings of ordinary life he would become an urban Robinson Crusoe. The fictional Crusoe however did not endure a life in solitary confinement. He could hold a conversation with another human being; Man Friday. Crusoe's archetype, Alexander Selkirk, had no such companion and the consequences were dire. Selkirk was a morose solitary Scot whose alienated shipmates abandoned him on the desert island of Más a Tierra in the Juan Fernández archipelago some hundreds of miles off the coast of Chile in the South Pacific. Selkirk survived alone for more than four years from 1704 to 1709. By then the long period of isolation had left its mark. People isolated from language learning from an early age, such as Victor of Aveyron, never achieve normal language skills and those kept in long isolation forget how to converse. After four years and four months of total isolation from another human being, Selkirk's rescuer, Captain Woodes Rogers the future governor of the Bahamas, recorded that Alexander Selkirk, was virtually incapable of speech.

Anthony, now with advanced dual sensory loss, saw little prospect of companionship as his constructed world fell apart. He had in some ways marooned himself through a lack of trust in others. Isolation can be the harshest form of imprisonment. Victorian prisons were designed to implement it in the form of the 'separate system' introduced in Britain under the 1839 Prisons Act. Prisoners were under constant surveillance. Reading Gaol was typical of the era. Even when attending chapel services inmates were put in cubicles to prevent eye contact[1]. It was intentionally cruel and enabled Reading's Gaol's most famous inmate, Oscar Wilde, to write one of his greatest works, *De Profundis.*

Anthony was not in a physical prison but his imagination had incarcerated him in one – and then he saw his means of escape; 'When I finally acknowledged my suppressed emotions the healing process began. I realised this was healthy and the family were my life line . . .'

25

Life lines

There are many forms of life lines. Family is one. Work another. Sailing proved an important third for Anthony. It came at the right time just as his tennis game was starting to decline. It served him well. When the last vestige of sight was leaving his eyes he did what came naturally to him and turned to help train RYA Disability volunteers.

'The idea of sailing never occurred to me in my youth. It happened during a casual conversation with a colleague at Berkshire County Council's Highway Department who said he was selling a dinghy. 'It's a Heron' he said. At that time I wouldn't have known a Heron from an Osprey unless you were talking about bird life but the idea of sailing sparked an immediate thrill and I jumped at the opportunity. The infant experience of drifting down the Lambourn River on a homemade raft with my father and elder brother had seared the thrill into my psyche. It turned out the Heron was an ideal boat for a complete novice. It is a 'one-design' craft that means any changes made to the boat for racing purposes are strictly regulated but there is some relaxation or 'leeway' in the non-nautical sense for personal tweaking. In later years I would become a master of fine tuning a boat. It almost became an obsession as I could happily spend too much time before and during a race tinkering with the rigging to harness its unique idiosyncrasies to maximise the boat's advantage.

For some sailors these fine adjustment may not make much difference to the outcome because they are gifted or conversely incompetent but when sailors are well matched the outcome will be affected by the ability of the helm to fine tune the boat and sail the racing line efficiently. Tuning was a vital issue for me because tunnel vision already disadvantaged me at the start line. Imagine a crowded start line of dinghies controlled by competitive helms who all want to win. The experienced ones will have jostled for the best position along the line while others might prefer to have momentum sailing behind the parked boats. The starting horn sounds and everyone frantically pulls in the main sheet allowing the sails to catch the wind. Those boats behind relying on momentum hope to push past those that are starting from a stationery position. Everyone is aiming for the first buoy and to capture the best line to it. Boats closest to the wind give way to those in the lee but no one is allowed to cause a collision. It can feel like chaos even for able sighted helms. But I am sailing in a surrounding fog with a small area of sharp focus in the centre of my vision. I am exhilarated. I know I can perform well provided my crew keep me informed of surrounding boats. My secret is attention to detail. Before the race I check every control on the boat. Sometimes I ask an experienced sailor to check my settings such as the bend in the mast and shroud tensions for example. Members are generally friendly and helpful – even at the start of the race when the adrenalin is kicking in. If I ignore these settings I will suffer because good sailors optimise their boats for speed before and throughout the race. Competing in a race is a responsible activity. There are so many things to think about and I know my limited sight will cause me to miss opportunities to gain tactical advantages. I cannot see changing cloud formations or shadows crossing the lake that indicate approaching gusts. I need to keep talking to my crew as this helps me form a changing picture of the race and our place in it.

My focus is on speed and I feel the movement of the boat. Right balance, right tension of the line in my hands. Boat and helm conjoined – a single entity. Unlike my competitors I cannot see the shape of the sail. People with vision can see how the sail is set. A perfectly shaped sail is smooth, unwrinkled and firm as opposed to flapping. It then becomes a streamlined aerofoil forcing the wind passing over the larger outside surface of the sail to travel faster. Lower pressure on the inside surface causes the boat to be sucked forward. Unfortunately the sucking force also produces unwanted sideways movement – the aforementioned leeway. Dinghies are therefore fitted with a centre board beneath the hull to stop the wind blowing the boat over and to resist sideways movement. The centre board and rudder counteract this force of the wind. These become a hindrance to speed however when the boat is sailing down wind and must be adjusted.

I feel the tension of the line in my hand to understand how the sail is behaving and listen to the crew. I run my hands along the foot of the boom to feel if the sail is double folded. I can often tell by touch if the sail is baggy. To ensure I'm on the right line for racing I rely on my sighted crew to tell me. I continually ask the crew how I am doing and the position of the buoy: talking all the time to give me a picture of our performance. The ability to compete in a talented fleet give me a sense of accomplishment and freedom I would otherwise not enjoy. It sometimes takes me out of a dark place.

Sailing plays to my strengths. Attention to detail is my strong point. I built a career on this discipline and it is what enables me to run a home without help as a deaf-blind person. It enables me to play chess, become an accomplished cook and participate in other competitive activities.'

Anthony quickly mastered the Heron and moved on to a more demanding dinghy. From his twenties onwards, however, tunnel vision would made it increasingly difficult to see changing cloud formations, approaching wind shadows and nearby competitors and he would increasingly rely on the eyes and ears of his crew and constant conversations. As his eyesight diminished the haptic sense of touch in his skin would enable him to feel the wind more acutely but this provided little compensation and poor eye sight always put him at a disadvantage to similarly talented helms.

Sailing was perhaps the ideal sport for him. It would draw on his athleticism and tactical mind, along with his aptitude for maths and engineering and formidable concentration but time would always be running out.

26

Heron, Enterprise and Challenger

'He didn't see me sneaking up but I could see the amazement in his face when he did and I was clearly an unwelcome intrusion. He was flying on a dead run but heading for the shore and veering away from the race line and the other dinghies. I could see him calculating the risk; jibe and cut across my path to stay in the race or shed wind and pass in my wake. Dilemma.

Well, I was too close now. He would have to let me pass. He was a strange helmsman, he kept moving his head about as if taking snap shots of the views around him. What was he thinking? There is a fine line between caution and foolhardiness and we were the larger vessel – a training boat full of students. I should have known there would be trouble. He was fuelled with adrenalin but I was under power but somehow we were both competing. I remember him and his crew shouting "water, water". Then suddenly the dinghy tried to jibe and pass across my path. The helm must have thought there was enough room.

Power gives way to sail. Rules of the road. But I was too close to apply this rule.'

'The adventure began when I took the newly acquired *Heron* down to Salcome along with my old school friend David. I remember the sense of excitement on seeing the aquamarine sea through the trees as I drove down into the town. There is something special about the hue of the sea here. Neither of us had a clue what to do but trusted in our abilities to work out how to set up the dinghy, solve problems and learn to sail through trial and error. Thankfully the *Heron* is a forgiving boat and we didn't capsize into the icy waters of the early summer estuary. On our return home we joined Reading Sailing Club. It was the mid-seventies and David to my surprise promptly purchased an Enterprise which is quite a handful for a novice sailor and I quickly followed his example.

The Enterprise is one of the main classes of dinghies found in sailing clubs. It is a four metre long dinghy with trade-mark light blue sails. The Class Association maintains strict rules to prevent unfair changes to the design of succeeding generations thus ensuring an older boat can perform competitively with a modern one. If you want to race seriously you need to be part of a class fleet to measure your competence against others in the same boat.

The 'Ent' as it is known has been around for a long time and has become a legend amongst dinghy sailors. The Class celebrated its 60th anniversary in 2016. The story began on January 9th 1956 when late one night two prototype Enterprise dinghies made an overnight crossing from Dover to Calais. It was a spectacular way to launch a performance dinghy whose cost would be within reach of most enthusiasts. Budgetary constraints led to a landmark innovation in modern mainsail rigging. A groove was fabricated in the mast for hoisting the sail and was strong enough to hold it under pressure. Until then expensive stainless steel shanks had been used. The groove is still the most common method of rigging today.

In the early eighties David and I moved to Burghfield Sailing

Club. This had a much bigger lake and better facilities although Reading Sailing Club would enlarge its lake and improve its facilities many years later after receiving a sizable grant from Sport England. I became fleet captain of the second largest fleet of 'Ents' in the country. I retained the captaincy for nine years and this remains my proudest accomplishment in terms of sailing. I spent a lot of time encouraging young sailors for as long as my sight would allow. Throughout this time the annual highlight was a week of competitive sailing off the South Coast. The venue offered Open Regatta racing for various classes of dinghy as well as World and National Championships.

Competitive racing is bound to cause collisions yet despite my limited vision I suffered no more accidents than able sighted competitors nor did I have any insurance refusals. In all this time I only suffered one serious accident and I still believe it was not my fault. I was sailing downwind in a race and needed to cross the path of a training boat using its engine. The boat was forcing me away from the next mark. If I was to retain a competitive place in the race I needed to pass in front of it. I shouted for some time and knew everyone on board could hear my yells for 'water' but the skipper chose to ignore me. I consulted with the crew and decided there was enough time to jibe and pass in front of the boat. I pulled in the main and thrust out the tiller turning the dinghy at right angles to the oncoming vessel.

Unfortunately my jibe was incompetent. The boat collided with us forcing us underwater as it sailed over the top. The hull probably saved both of us from fatal injuries. I suspect the skipper was thinking he could bully us aside by ignoring the rules of sailing. It was an uncomfortable brush with mortality and our dinghy suffered heavy damage. I challenged the skipper but he refused to acknowledge his error. He knew he was guilty. I could have taken him to court for putting lives at risk but what would a jury think when they discover that I am partially sighted and have a 70 decibel hearing loss? It could have become complicated and expensive. Furthermore the skipper was young and probably inexperienced and so I dropped it. Just move on.

Around 2002 my sight was continuing to deteriorate and Chrissie was crewing less and less due to the impact of a double organ transplant. Start lines were becoming particularly harrowing as twenty competitive boats jostled for position in strong gusty winds as the clock ran down to the start. During the race I increasingly relied on my crew to tell me the position of the approaching buoys and I spent a lot of time in the water as I insisted on sailing the Enterprise to its limits. At this point my sailing ambitions would have come to an end had it not been for two useful developments at the club. My continuation was made possible by the Royal Yachting Association's (RYA) Sailability[1]. This is the RYA's national programme enabling people with disabilities to learn to sail and compete. It has accredited facilities in many clubs across the UK and its aim is to advance education and promote the welfare of disabled people and encourage their participation. They provide a number of specially adapted boats and at Burghfield were able to offer me a Challenger which is a single-handed trimaran with a mainsail'.

The Class specifically allows disabled people to sail independently and on equal terms with able-bodied sailors and is competitive in most club racing fleets. It does not heel or capsize and has the option of an electric servo and can be used by people with poor upper body strength and balance. It is self-bailing so any water splashing into the cockpit is automatically removed.

Despite being an unsinkable boat it is capable of providing the excitement of competitive racing and optional electronic controls and personalized seating add to its suitability for severely disabled helms. I was impressed with Sailability and spent a lot of time on its committee'.

Anthony used to compete in Enterprise Open meetings across the country. Now with the help of his brother, Christopher, he began attending Challenger Opens where he was often the only blind sailor. At Grafton Water in Cambridgeshire Christopher was in the safety boat following Anthony. The boats were manoeuvring for position at the start line when Anthony suddenly turned his boat and headed for the shore. Christopher was surprised by this uncharacteristic withdrawal and followed.

Despite tunnel vision he could detect 'a very angry black storm cloud' approaching. He sensed its threat and was concerned his latest hearing aid could be ruined if he capsized. While putting away the boat the storm suddenly arrived toppling a number of disabled sailors into the lake. The wind was so strong that even uncapsizable Challengers were turned over. The ferocity of the storm only lasted for around thirty minutes but the risk of disabled sailors becoming entangled in the rigging of upturned boats stirred the safety boats into urgent action. Anthony, who never abandons races, explained later that he was deeply disturbed by the presence of the cloud and decided to get off the water while he still had an opportunity.

He thought his sailing days were coming to an end but just when the last vestiges of his sight were dimming, rather than surrender to the inevitable, he made his own unique contribution to dinghy sailing. He set out to produce a system that would enable blind people to sail competitively without the support of a sighted crew member.

In November 2006 and approaching his 60th birthday Anthony contacted a marine publication for its help in the search for a company to develop a system. He had spoken to several people in the industry but none were aware of anything capable of meeting his requirements. He contacted a specialist marine company in Cornwall which had been working on a related project. The company had already developed suitable technology. His idea to devise a guidance system for blind sailors had come about when he was invited to join a British crew in an Anglo-Italian Match Racing championship.

'This gave me the opportunity to experience a higher realm of disability sailing. I was still sailing competitively at Burghfield when I received the invitation to join a team competing against the Italians at The Blind Match Racing World Championship in Sonar dinghies. Match sailing is a competition between two boats racing around a circuit. The Sonar one-design keelboat is a high-performance 23 foot racing dinghy and crewed by four people; a helm, two crew members to control the main sheet and jib and a sighted safety officer who is not allowed to influence the team's performance other than to protect them from danger.

I remember the event was hosted at the Queen Mary Sailing Club in May 2000. The format consisted of two British and two Italian teams. Since there were only two boats in the race it was possible to use an acoustic system to identify the start line which emitted a single sound to port side and double sound to the starboard. Three buoys equipped with an acoustic signal enabled us to locate our targets and follow the upwind and downwind legs of the course. There was also an acoustic sound to identify both dinghies. Once we were well into the race however I found the various signals confusing and often muffled by the wind and this detracted from the joy of sailing. Nevertheless I was determined to make the best of it.

We won and the trophy was presented by the Chief Executive of the charity Action for the Blind. The event was reported in the 9 June 2000 edition of *Yachts and Yachting* where I appear in a photograph with the other two crew members.

The limitations of the acoustic system gave me the idea of developing a system that would enable totally blind people to race dinghies competitively without the array of pulsed sounds being emitted. It would be a type of simple GPS emitting short messages such as 'buoy port side 200 metres' . . .buoy portside 1000 metres'. The search for a specialised company led me to Cornwall and the result was the 'Sailguide' system which was fitted to a thirty-five foot yacht for sea trials'.

The first time Anthony rounded a buoy unaided was a deeply memorable moment. The culmination of so much effort. He had succeeded. He burst into tears as did others witnessing the moment as he realised he had at last achieved the objective of solo blind sailing. The system was subsequently transferred to his Challenger trimaran. The dinghy being so much smaller than the yacht however made it difficult to maintain the equipment when stored in a boat yard. The computer system (GPS) had to be removed and the battery disconnected. The system needed further development but without outside investment, costs were becoming too much for one person.

'The day I tested the Sailguide system was a wonderful and emotional experience. It was the first time since becoming blind that I was able to sail without assistance. I thought I would never realise my ambition of sailing independently again but this gave me hope that one day I would race again. I had wanted to develop a system that would indicate the presence of other boats in a fleet but this was a complex technological challenge and by now I was running out of money and more importantly Chrissie was becoming quite ill with cancer'.

The personal endeavour had come to an end and it wasn't long before smart-phone companies were developing apps enabling the blind to sail yachts on the sea but even these giants had yet to crack the problem of unaided blind competitive fleet racing. I had seen a better world for blind sailors but perhaps I was too ambitious'.

27

Rumour and the Vision

Professor Jones warmed the glass of brandy in his hands and allowed the ambience of Wales' grandest hotel to comfort him. 'It's interesting that we can study the beginnings of history 46 billion light years ago in the remotest part of the cosmos and yet the history of this place doesn't allow us to agree what happened a mere 300 years ago Tom'.

'Well, I'm sure the records will eventually come to life professor'. It was late and Tom was too tired to spark yet another conversation about a new subject.

The Cambridge professor of astrophysics was visiting with his family. They had retired to bed leaving the professor and his friend to enjoy the remains of the evening.

As midnight approached, the professor looked across the bay to the twinkling lights of a ship far out to sea and listened to the soft roar of the waves disintegrating on the beach. As he admired the view he was mildly surprised to think that while he worked in eons of time, this place had been transformed from wild marshland in less than three centuries. How quickly the resort had grown, reached its apogee and now reclined in the reflected glory of its past. For a short time it had been one of Europe's most fashionable seaside resorts welcoming heads of state. It all happened in the blink of an eye. Cosmically speaking.

Tom stood next to him looking out at the same infinity of dark sea and sky. 'It is said that the story of Llandudno as a resort began in 1846 when a

Liverpool surveyor, Owen Williams, visited the town with his friend, John Williams. Not much seems to be known about John or why he came here other than that he was a businessman and needed to attend a meeting of shareholders of the local copper mine' . . .

The day had begun cloudy but the town was now domed by a sun-filled sky and fragrance of the sea. Since John Williams would be engaged with the mine's shareholders until late after-noon Owen had the whole day to himself. He had agreed to meet John for dinner in the King's Head and so to pass the time Owen walked around the town that was really little more than a village with a population of less than a thousand souls. It was during this walk that it happened. It was just a momentary insight as he admired the beautiful contour of the bay and soft uninter-rupted beach. Some might call it mystical; as when Wordsworth reflected on Tintern Abbey but whereas this led Wordsworth to write poetry Owen's reflection led him to think of surveying. The vision agitated him and he grew impatient to see his friend in the evening. When the two sat down to dinner Owen was in an excited frame of mind and eager to plant the seed of an idea that would transform the small town and marshlands forever.

'I have had the most wonderful, most inspiring apprehen-sion John'.

'Wonderful apprehension. Isn't that a contraction Owen?

'No John for I have determined that if this vision be given me I must act upon it without delay but with all due caution too, you understand'.

'You confound me Owen I must say. One minute you speak of this and then of that. Come, come sir what is it that so excites you?'

'A vision John. I had a vision as strong as today's sunlight. I saw nothing less than the future of this place. What do you see here John?'

'Marshland sir'.

'Yes but this is marshland that can easily be drained and out of its silt a new and marvellous bathing resort will arise'.

This story of the fashionable Victorian seaside resort of Llandudno enters Anthony's family history because the Kings Head, where John and Owen had dinner, was owned by Anthony's great, great, maternal grandfather William Owen (alas details of his wife are missing from the family archive). Their only surviving child, Anne Jane Owen, married Isaiah Davies whose family had significant business interests in the area. They owned a farm and held shares in a copper mine; both located on the Great Orme. Isaiah and Anne later inherited the King's Head Inn, reputed to be the oldest pub in Llandudno.

This would be a tenuous family link to the rise of the seaside resort had it not been for Isaiah being an ambitious man. Having married Anne at the age of nineteen he went on to build the most significant property on the seafront, the St George's Hotel, by the age of twenty four.

Annie Mary Davies, possibly their second child, was born in 1850. She married Thomas Jameson October 1877 at the age of twenty one. The Marriage Certificate describes her as of the St George's Hotel in the parish of Llandudno. Thomas Jameson had been raised by an uncle on a small farm at Ellerton cum Brantingham, Yorkshire and moved to Liverpool. How Thomas met Annie is not clear but after the marriage the couple settled in Liverpool to start a new chapter in the Lawton story.

Meanwhile the St George's Hotel (an unusual name for a prominent and famous Welsh establishment) quickly rose in prominence attracting European royalty and heads of state. These included Napoleon III and his wife Princess Eugenie, Count Otto Von Bismarck, Queen Elizabeth of Romania and a series of British Prime Ministers such as Benjamin Disraeli, William Ewart Gladstone, Winston Churchill and David Lloyd George and more recently John Major and Tony Blair. Margaret Thatcher is rumoured to have launched her career here.

Alas, Owen Williams did not write about his existential experience until the 1880s. Since this was many years after the development of the resort during the years 1857 to 1877 following the appointment of the surveyor and architect George Felton it remains anecdotal. What is known, is that Owen submitted a detailed proposal to the Honourable Edward Mostyn, 2nd Baron Mostyn in 1847 which created two competing futures: a commercial port or a fashionable bathing resort. The resort won and the seaside town of Llandudno rose out of the marshes of Morfa Rhianedd along with Lawton family's own apocryphal chapter in history.

28

Lawton's Liverpool

The DNA that shaped Anthony Lawton is a rich Victorian mixture of Norfolk, Yorkshire, Lancashire and north Welsh origin. If taken further back the lineage might reveal a few foreign interventions along with saints and darker characters whose nefarious dealings are long shrouded by the mists of time. The genetic patterns that cascade through Anthony's ancestors of Owen, Jameson, Evans, Reed and Neves, Lawton and Shaw, like all genetic patterns, are harbingers of advantage and disadvantage: certainty and uncertainty. In Anthony's case two faulty genes had randomly come together somewhere in history to bestow hearing loss and severe retinal dysfunction. The genetic question was asked by a consultant ophthalmologist at the John Radcliffe Eye Hospital in Oxford in 2019 when between outbreaks of Covid-19 Anthony participated in research. He was a willing guinea pig. He vaguely recalls the question: ' . . . with RP the mother is always the carrier. Do you have distant cousins in the family who married? I ask because it requires two compatible genes to trigger the condition and the chances of this happening are extremely unlikely'. Anthony thinks silently ' . . . or extremely unlucky'. Who were the cousins? A tantalising clue lurks in a corner of the graveyard on the Great Orme . . .

The Lawton family tree[1], like most family histories is difficult to piece together as many names intertwine, disappear out of sight or reappear later in the story. Thomas and Annie Jameson had nine children and the Lawton name enters Anthony's story when Gwendoline Thomas Jameson, their seventh child, married Thomas Lawton on the 4 July 1914. Gwendoline and Thomas had three children Joseph, Ellinor and Gwennie – who would become Anthony's mother. Gwendoline died giving birth to Gwennie in 1920.

Thomas and Annie Jameson's eighth child, Eric Jameson[2], married Flora Reed and had three children, Pauline, Robert and Gordon. Pauline Isobel Jameson went on to become a well-known actress on film and stage. She was talent spotted at the Colwyn Bay Repertory Company in 1938 and offered a role in a West End play which she followed up with a series of successful seasons at the Old Vic Company and Shakespeare Festival Theatre, Stratford. She simultaneously developed a prolific film career acting alongside Laurence Oliver, Dirk Bogarde, Tony Hancock and Judy Garland. She resumed her acting career after the premature death of her husband, Wing Commander Leslie Lewington, and made various appearances in the popular TV series, *Poirot*.

Flora Reed's brother, Bill, performed in another arena and managed or owned the national construction company, Reed & Malik where Cedric, Anthony's uncle trained to become a professional civil engineer. Cedric had won a scholarship to King's Lynn Grammar School and Bill would later fund John who would otherwise not have been accepted here. There still exists a reference publication about the Reed & Malik Company in the Bodleian Library at the University of Oxford. Two of the Reed's daughters ran a bakery in Rhuddlan North Wales where Cedric worked briefly. In 1934 he cycled home to spend Christmas with his family in Norfolk and after telling stores of his adventures discovered that John wanted to cycle back with him. John was offered work as a baker's boy delivering bread and it was through this activity that he probably met Gwennie Lawton.

The crux of the Lawton-Shaw parental story however is based in Liverpool. It begins with the troubled birth of Gwennie, who might have perished with her mother had it not been for some inspired nursing in 1920. There is an apocryphal tale that Gwennie's father, Thomas Lawton was an unhappy man who came to despise his daughter, holding her responsible for the death of his wife; an accusation she was not able to challenge or escape throughout her childhood. According to family legend she was a spirited child and frequently in trouble; strong willed and determined.

Thomas remarried quite quickly and produced a daughter Jane, although the name of her mother appears to have been lost from the records. Gwennie did not enjoy a good relationship with her stepmother who ignored her emotional needs and those of her older sister Ellinor and brother Joseph. Despite this indifference Gwennie enjoyed a close relationship with her new half-sister whom she came to cherish. She was also close to her Lawton grandparents receiving their affection and generosity and benefited from the advantages of these years. She attended private schools and was chauffeured around Liverpool in the family Bentley often with the grandparents she loved. The family home was a grand four-storey building set beside the landscaped 200 acre Sefton Park to the south of the city centre. The park with its distinctive watercourses and sculptures provided temporary escapes for the girls especially when Thomas became drunk and the parents descended into fierce and potentially dangerous arguments. Today Sefton Park is a restored Grade 1 historic park. Its famous glasshouse survived both the Blitz and post-war decline and was restored after many years to recapture the original awe-inspiring intentions of its Victorian designers. When Gwennie and Christopher visited the area decades after leaving it they were saddened to see the surrounding suburb was a pale reflection of its affluent past.

According to one source (Gracesguide.co.uk), J.A. Lawton and Co (Coachbuilders) was founded in 1870 in Liverpool by Joseph Alfred Lawton. The company started to manufacture coachworks for a car company in the early 1900s and opened a factory in London. There is a family anecdote that Morris Motors Limited offered to go into Partnership with J.A. Lawton & Co to build cars but Thomas rejected the approach. By such decisions are fortunes lost or made. This story will probably remain apocryphal although there are certainly connections between the car manufacturing names of Whitlock, J.A. Lawton and Lawton-Goodman. When the company formed a London connection it changed from J.A. Lawton & Co to the London Carriage Company and the showroom in Hope Street became the London Carriage Works. Today the premises, built in the architectural Venetian palazzo fashion of the 1860s, have become a fashionable restaurant 'The London Carriage works'. The name was discovered carved in the stone lintel above the main entrance during a renovation and retained out of respect for the building's history. Few restaurants can boast such an idiosyncratic pedigree.

Thomas Owen Alfred Lawton had joined the company at the

age of seventeen and became responsible for managing it. He was ill equipped to take on the task and would have had little or no training at a time when the nascent British car industry was impacting the manufacture of carriages. Technology, manufacturing methods and management processes were changing much faster than they had in the past. Thomas received poor business advice and his decisions put the company into crisis. He became an alcoholic and struggling with business and personal issues, Thomas Lawton and the once thriving but now debt-ridden Lawton Carriage Company collapsed.

Grandfather Joseph Alfred Lawton became disillusioned with Thomas, who according to family anecdotes, succumbed to violent and drunken outbursts in the workplace. When the drunken rages became too much, Gwennie, her brother Joseph and sisters lived temporarily with their nearby grandparents and returned when safe. Gwennie vividly remembered an occasion when driving through Liverpool with her grandfather, the chauffeur, Ladmore, spotted Thomas on the street, evidently drunk. Ladmore said 'look sir, there's young Mr Lawton, should I stop?' Grandfather Lawton sternly told him to drive on. It was a painful moment for everyone. When the business failed the family home was sold. Thomas Lawton was undoubtedly under a lot of pressure in an era that was experiencing unprecedented industrial change.

Gwennie also stayed with her uncle Noel and aunt Ellinor Evans (nee Lawton) in their spacious house in Harlech, North Wales. They showed kindness to the children in unexpected ways such as setting up saving trusts. Lewis Noel Vincent Evans was High Sherriff of Merionethshire and a pillar of the community. Lewis was an Englishman and his grave is marked by an English oak cross in Harlech cemetery amongst a sea of Welsh slate. He died 9 February 1967. Christopher Lawton and his brothers continue to tend his grave periodically and boast that it is the only St Georges Cross in Wales. There is another family grave in the cemetery on the Great Orme, Llandudno. It is found just to the left of the arched entrance to the new extension where the ashes of Ellinor Neves, Gwennie's sister, are buried after being flown over from Canada. Gwennie's ashes out of respect for her wishes were later scattered on Harlech Beach. The cemetery provides another mystery in the family's interwoven intergenerational relationships. During his childhood Anthony and his family would visit a large mausoleum; that of the Willis Family. Who were they? No connections have been made and Anthony and his brothers have no idea who they were or why they visited? Does the cemetery hold a clue to the distant cousins who married? The family history appendices show that Eric Jameson is Gwennie Lawton's uncle and John Shaw's grandfather. They are cousins but it is impossible to know if the distaff line carried the defective genes that trigger retinitis pigmentosa or Ushers Syndrome type 2'.[2]

The search for the cousins who may have triggered the legacy of genetic disease is shrouded in vaguely remembered personal history and anecdotal theory and ancestral searches are fraught with difficulties. Records are not infallible, sometimes they are incomplete and open to interpretation. Who are the missing people? The Eastern Daily Press ran an article on Tuesday 4 March 2003 with the story of a woman in Birmingham who had discovered a long-lost sister and believes her mother is Sylvia Reed. The article includes a childhood photograph with Mrs Reed. According to the family tree however Sylvia was single and died in 1988 but this could be misleading. Research for this memoir has been limited to the more easily accessible records. Not all possibilities have been explored and this leaves room for the Lawton-Shaw story to be developed by future generations.

29

The White Sweater

'In 1920 my paternal grandfather, John Arthur Shaw moved the family from Bexley Heath in London to Heacham, south-east Norfolk. John had three brothers. Geoffrey the eldest was six at this time and suffering from consumption and poor eye sight and was the reason for the move away from London. My father, Arthur John Shaw (John) was four and Eldred two. The youngest brother Cedric was born shortly after the move to Norfolk. The family rented a house, 'Primrose House' which provided spacious accommodation and two acres of land. It was a paradise for my father and his brothers as it contained a walnut tree, orchard and duck pond. There was a bungalow at the far end where Evelyn Alice Shaw (née Reed) John's grandmother lived. My grandfather was cold and aloof but grandmother was warm and loving. Geoffrey was admitted to the sanatorium in the nearby village of Holt and the other boys attended the local Elm Village School.

My grandfather turned down the opportunity to purchase the house because he believed it was better for the landlord to pay for its upkeep and they moved to a modern semi-detached property called 'Fernleigh' where Eldred died aged ten of meningitis. He was cherished and gifted and the loss was to have a lasting impact on the family. Years later when John's mother commissioned the building of a bungalow near Fernleigh it was named Eldred Bungalow and I was christened Anthony Eldred Shaw in memory of the lost boy and missing uncle.

My father initially prospered in Heacham. At the age of twelve his uncle, Bill Reed, paid for his education at the prestigious King's Lynn grammar school since he lacked the appropriate entrance qualification. At this point however he seems to have lost his way and gained the reputation of a tearaway. The reason remains a family mystery but a white sweater is the key suspect. Although the school fees were covered by his uncle the family were left to supply his equipment and parsimony is suspected for the failure to provide a school uniform. His mother knitted him a white sweater causing him to stand out in a sea of blazers and school ties. It would have been known that he lacked the academic attainment for a free education and in the highly class-conscious era of the late nineteen twenties and thirties the jumper would mark him out as an outsider. He no doubt suffered daily taunts and bullying as I would too decades later. The headmaster had no regard for John who simply nurtured romantic dreams of becoming an RAF pilot. He left school empty handed without as much as a good reference. Cedric qualified for school entrance and was a much more measured student and later pursued a career in civil engineering. Geoffrey was discharged from the sanatorium at the age of fifteen and became involved in the family business of refurbishing organs and pianos. A few years later he moved to Rhuddlan in North Wales to help in a bakery attached to a café operated by two of his maternal great aunts. He returned to Heacham on a bike to celebrate Christmas with the family in 1933. During this time he spun various tales of adventures motivating John to return with him to north Wales where he found employment delivering loaves to customers. At this time a family relative from Liverpool, Gwennie Lawton, moved to Rluddlan and the couple must have met and visited that city because it was there that John responded to a street recruitment campaign in 1935 and joined the RAF.

Geoffrey and Cedric were prevented from joining up at the outbreak of war due to poor eye sight and ill health and Geoffrey remained in Rhuddlan. He returned to Heacham after the war and bought a house in Neville Road. He lived out his life here with his family and was given a share in the family business. Many years later I read a letter written by my father recalling his school years and the head master's hostility. By now he had a senior role in NATO and based in Germany. He reflected on his prospects at the age of sixteen and after the war. He wrote that his achievement 'would have knocked my old head teacher off his chair'.

30

John's War

Anthony reads a letter from his father who is currently stationed in Monchengladbach. It is the 1960s and John, who is not permitted to visit his sons, wants them to know about his wartime experiences. Private stories fit into bigger narratives that change families, shape the world and squeeze populations into the anonymity of suffering. It is early morning 1 September, 1939. Corporal John Shaw is enjoying breakfast in silent thought in the clattering canteen of RAF Hucknell. Only the ocassional sound of steel pots falling to the ground penetrate his thoughts. A soft cocooning babble of voices echo in the recess of his consciousness. It is the start of another quiet day. Every day is quiet. Sunlight daubs diaphanous patterns on the canteen windows and he reflects on his chances of selection for pilot training. Meanwhile 900 miles away, the Nazi invasion of Poland has begun and ill-equipped Polish armed services in forward positions reel under the fire power of the Wehrmacht military machine.

John's journey to RAF Hucknell began in 1935 when he saw an RAF recruitment parade marching towards him. He had only recently professed his love for a woman who was his social superior yet his need for adventure trumped. His response was impulsive and he was sent to RAF Cranwell for basic training

barely having time to wave goodbye. Although he lacked qualifications to become a pilot he would find a way. His first posting was RAF Bircham Newton in his home county of Norfolk
and then a year later, RAF Seletar in Singapore where he arrived
as a fully qualified wireless operator hungry for the unknown.
RAF Seletar operated one of the most technologically advanced
aircraft of its era; the six-crew Short Sunderland flying boat.
John was part of a crew undertaking maritime reconnaissance
missions. Sunderlands were the only aircraft capable of flying
long range reconnaissance missions at this time. One day in
the future Australian crews operating these flying boats
from an RAF base in Devon would save the life of his first son,
Christopher.

Singapore was an idyllic posting and John made the most of it
visiting Borneo, Malaysia and the Nicobar Islands. He travelled
with a group of RAF friends including Gunner Sergeant Pat
Patmore who, eight years later in 1945, having survived years
of enslavement on the Burmese Railway, would perish on a
Japanese ship transporting POWs. It would be attacked by a US
aircraft. Before the outbreak of war John had learnt to fly a single-
seater biplane at Seletar. This would have been either the Sopwith
Pup or Tiger Moth. This experience and the endorsement
of his commanding officer (possibly Squadron Leader
C. H. Flinn) provided the ticket back to Britain for pilot selection.
Then in August 1939 he was promoted to Corporal and posted
to RAF Hucknall in the East Midlands where he would excel
in training Polish pilots in the use of aircraft communication
systems. It was both a modest step up the chain of command
and a move in the wrong direction – taking him away from pilot
training.

At RAF Hucknall John is employed in the Signals Section (wireless operation) under the command of No 12 Group Headquarters. They work around the clock using a three-watch system and John is responsible for a team of teleprinter operators. Each teleprinter is linked to an operational station in the group. The work is tediously routine especially when bad weather restricts flights and this demands a different type of discipline from the watch leader. Boredom eats into John's consciousness. He cannot be bored because to be bored risks day dreaming. Outside the window more exciting possibilities fill his imagination and pass him by. He has a tedious responsibility. Managing this reliably means he could manage more complex operations tomorrow. But for now in the Signals operation room at Hucknall he is one of many essential conjoining synapses in the neural network of Fighter Command. Any malfunctions at Hucknall would create exploitable weaknesses in the command, control, and communication capability of the RAF.

In the bitterly cold winter of 1940 aircraft are grounded, airwaves are silent and inactivity is endured while far away populations bleed out of Eastern Europe. The RAF base is silent but watchful as the Battle of Britain approaches. It will arrive on 10 July 1940. In the mining village of Hucknall where events rarely happen, apart from Saturday night brawls outside the dance hall, the pub landlord and local fish and chip shop proprietor are deliriously happy, as is the manager of the one and only cinema. The RAF has become the second major employer in the town and its employees eat the one establishment empty and drink the other dry. The mining community is not happy.

Far away from these minor frictions, history is unravelling in Poland due to its agreement to the recriminatory conditions of the Treaty of Versailles of 1919. Its acquiescence invites the Fuhrer's wrath and the Third Reich prepares to deliver annihilation. The German attack is so swift the world's fourth largest military power with outmoded weaponry finds itself unable to mobilise effectively. Just sixteen days later the Polish government flees to Romania and on 17 September and in accordance with the Molotov–Ribbentrop Pact Soviet Russia invades Poland and the planned partition of the country is complete. Over 6,000 Polish soldiers die on the Russian front and hundreds of thousands are taken prisoner. The numbers rise with the subsequent annexation of the Baltic States where around 70,000 are interned. It is estimated that more than 1.5 million Poles are captured and deported to die in captivity.

By 18th September 1939 Siły Powietrzne units (Polish Air Force, PAF) trapped in Poland along with other Polish Forces manage to break through the Prut Valley and along the Jablonkow Pass in the Carpathian Mountains to Hungary. There are no formal diplomatic ties or agreements with Hungary and so these service personnel expect harsher treatment compared to their compatriots who had reached Romania. They arrive in tatters and to their surprise sympathetic Hungarians help 100,000 soldiers and PAF Units escape the clutches of the Gestapo.

The British, French and the Polish Government in exile meet in Paris in October 1939 to discuss how the redundant Polish forces can be utilised. The Poles want in particular to re-establish their air force in Britain where they had been trained and have a high regard for RAF equipment. The British and a former Air Attaché in Warsaw see an opportunity to use Polish navigators to fill a shortfall in the RAF's resources.

The evacuation of such a large number of people is only possible because of the sympathies of neighbouring countries who once formed the pre-war 'Little Entente' that included Czechoslovakia, Hungary,

Romania and more tenuously Yugoslavia. Although the now defunct Entente was created to prevent a Hapsburg resurgence in central Europe the underlying bonds of friendship remain amongst the people. When Polish forces cross their borders they are interned in camps but encouraged to escape. In Hungary an undercover network enables over 30,000 Poles to be smuggled into Yugoslavia. British and French legations in Bucharest subsequently help General Zajac, the commander of the PAF, organise the evacuation of over 90,000 personnel from the Romanian camps. Escalation of the war and growing political pressure means that by the end of 1939 the escape routes are effectively controlled by the Gestapo. The evacuation however is meticulously planned enabling internees to escape in civilian clothing with the right documentation despite Germany's growing insistence that these smaller nations contain the Poles in their camps until Germany can decide their fate.

The destiny of the escaping PAF however is precarious. Those fleeing to Latvia find temporary refuge in internment camps but not many escape to France via Sweden and Norway. The majority are moved to Soviet gulags run by the notorious NKVD secret police where they perish. The treachery of 'Operation Barbarossa' in June 1941 when Germany invades Russia shifts the balance of power again and London encourages diplomatic relations to be restored with Poland. Tens of thousands of surviving Polish prisoners-of-war are now released on the understanding that they are allies of the Soviet Union subordinate to the Polish government-in-exile.

Escape routes that, one way or another, lead to the Black Sea enable evacuees to travel through Syria or Malta to reach France and Britain. An alternative route leads to Split in Yugoslavia and then to France by ship. Others escape to Piraeus in Greece while others simply walk to freedom through Yugoslavia and northern Italy. Some cross through Germany and the Low Countries but many cross the Carpathian Mountains where a multitude of trails reach an apogee in the wild uplands where a large *number of caves enable the Resistance to help escapees throughout the war and enrich the folklore of the Goralé*.

By 1940 around 35,000 members of the Polish armed forces have reached Britain including some 8,500 airmen. Many do not speak English and the urgent challenge for the RAF is to turn them into operational squadrons capable of supporting the war effort. The creation of a Polish Operations Training Unit[1] at RAF Hucknall ends eight long months of boredom for Corporal John Shaw when in March 1940 he is assigned to a special team of instructors to train Polish bomber crews. The Fairey Battle three-seat, single engine aircraft is used for training purposes. It is an outdated but indispensable light bomber. John is specifically responsible for the wireless section associated with one of the three Flights forming the unit. A Flight is the name given to a group of three to six aircraft including their aircrews and ground staff.

In 1940 he resumes flying as the Squadron Commander's wireless operator and is delighted to be in the air again for the first time since leaving Singapore. Then after only two months the Commander recommends him for a commission in the newly formed Technical Branch of the RAF where he would become a Signals Officer. John fails to value the opportunity as his heart is set on becoming a pilot much to the Squadron Commander's chagrin and is invited to attend the Air Crew Selection Centre at RAF Cardington. Although John has trained on a bi-plane in Singapore, completed a Navigation course, gained a Higher Education Test and is one of six airmen of the Far Eastern Command who had been recommended for Sergeant Pilot training, he is rejected without reason. It might be that his knowledge of Signals is considered more valuable to the RAF.

No airborne occupation is safe during the war years and when flying as a wireless operator he experiences many near-misses with death. The first came when accompanying his Squadron Commander. The aircraft was approaching Birmingham shortly after a German bombing raid and the pilot failed to see barrage balloons obscured by columns of black smoke rising from the city. On another occasion a Polish pilot who was not cleared to fly also failed to see a balloon cable as he flew along a Welsh beach and narrowly avoided a collision. John also risked death by refusing to wear a parachute due to the uncomfortably small wireless operator's chair. This proved to be a mistake when another Polish pilot flew down a narrow valley shrouded in mist until rocks appeared before them. The pilot's evasive action threw John from his seat and sent him sliding towards an opening in the fuselage. He managed to hold on at the last moment as his parachute plunged out of the aircraft.

John was then promoted to sergeant and moved to RAF Bramcote six miles from Coventry and again narrowly avoids obliteration by a stray bomb the night the city is reduced to a firestorm. The attack could have been countered if the newly operational Bletchley Park had alerted Fighter Command but the information was not released for reasons of national security. John continues to train Polish pilots, navigators and wireless operators throughout 1940 and is later given higher level responsibility in the Signals Training Section. He is introduced to a new radio system being developed for large aircraft at the Marconi works in Chelmsford as well as preparing wireless operators for the 'One Thousand Bomber' raids. The purpose of such a large fleet was to impress the enemy with the number of planes available to bomb German cities. This necessitated the use of obsolete aircraft. This strategy was later changed to focus on efficiency rather than high numbers. By now John is dissatisfied with his role in Signals and tries through subterfuge to join one of the bombing sorties. His subterfuge is discovered however and he is severely reprimanded for reckless behaviour. That night Polish bomber crews suffer one of their heaviest losses of the war.

In 1941 John marries Gwennie who joins him at Bramcote and they live off camp in nearby Nuneaton. Later that year John receives a further promotion to the rank of Flight Sergeant. In the spring of the following year their first son, Christopher is born on 20 April 1942. All is going well until he receives an unexpected order from his former Signals Officer in Singapore who persuades him to apply to the Technical Branch without delay. John complies and training begins 7 September 1942 at RAF Cosford. This marks the end of training aircrew but before leaving a member of the Polish aristocracy presents him with a tribute on behalf of Polish aircrews under his instruction.

On 8 October 1942 John is moved to RAF Mount Batten, a coastal command station near Plymouth as an officer in the Technical Branch where he shares a mess with two other recently commissioned officers. Australian aircrews stationed here operate Sunderland Flying Boats. The crews are unfriendly but attitudes change when they learn that John was once a wireless officer in Sunderlands in Singapore. At this time Christopher becomes ill with an unusual dietary condition treatable only by ingesting bananas. Since these are unobtainable in wartime Britain the Australians, on hearing of the emergency, arrange a banana run from Gibraltar and so save his life. During this time at Mount Batten John receives automatic promotion to Flying Officer.

Then in March 1943 John's life changes when he is made part of a secret operation. The team is accommodated in a temporary camp in Morecambe and issued with Mepacrine tablets to guard against malaria. One of the team refuses to take the tablets boasting of his immunity to the disease which kills him some months later. Morecambe provides a brief respite filled with leisurely walks in the Lancashire coastal countryside but this ends abruptly with orders to pack and be ready to board a night troop train to an unknown destination. He sails from Glasgow aboard the US ship, SS *Argentina*, on 10 May 1943 escorted by two naval destroyers. His ship is headed for Freetown, the capital of Sierra Leone, on the West Coast of Africa and will travel via Gibraltar.

Unfortunately after leaving' Gibraltar the destroyer escorts are diverted leaving the troop ship vulnerable to attack. His mood is lightened however when invited to join officers in a gourmet restaurant. John hopes to be promoted to Signals Officer in charge of a squadron but is posted to the British HQ in Freetown. He escapes malaria but is bought down with pneumonia and is moved to an army hospital located on a hillside 1,000 feet above sea level. He is here for a month and it is a cool and relaxing place to recover. During this time he is offered the post of 'Signal 3' and promoted to Acting Flight Lieutenant.

Freetown is a naval base. The British Army has long moved out and on 1 July 1943 John is moved to a new hillside HQ a mile outside the city. HQ consists of Wing Commander, Squadron Leader three Flight Lieutenants one of whom is a Canadian Air

Force radar specialist. Since the war is moving away from West Africa John has an opportunity to travel to other group HQs in Gambia and Nigeria flying in a cold Dakota aircraft. As Acting Flight Lieutenant he takes charge of three projects. The first is on the Italian battleship *Luigi di Savoia Duca Degli Abruzzi* which had surrendered to the British in Freetown Harbour. John's project is to brief the Italian Signals Officer about the RAF system of aircraft direction finding. The second project gives him a key technical role calibrating a Direction Finding (DF) station for the future airport of Freetown which is being built by the RAF. Unfortunately this required frequent hazardous journeys overland including a ninety-minute river crossing. Everyone carries a rifle. A final project was to provide the greatest satisfaction since it required John's unique experience with radio equipment. The West African coast is blighted with sudden and violent storms originating in the foothills of mountains 200 miles inland. These are then funnelled towards the coast causing chaos for ships and aircraft unaware of imminent and dramatic changes in the weather. John oversees the building of a portable wireless station in the compound of the District Commissioner's residence at Kabala some 150 miles inland. It will be manned by two wireless operators trained in meteorological forecasting.

John Shaw's active service ended in September 1944 and for unknown reasons he managed avoid joining the continuing war against Japan.' He returned to the UK and after four brief RAF postings across England was offered a permanent commission in the Technical Branch based at RAF Jurby on the Isle of Man. Shortly afterwards he received a certificate signed by the Secretary of State for Air stating he had been mentioned in a Despatch for Distinguished Service acknowledging 'His Majesty's high appreciation.' This was reported in the *London Gazette* on 1 January 1945.

*Carpathian highlanders

31

Gwennie's War

Gwennie is running through the dark. It is 2.00am, 1 May 1941 and the Liverpool Blitz has begun. There are no street lights and no light from surrounding windows to help her on her way. She steps around fire hoses and the debris of bombed and burning buildings. Far above is the distressing drone of enemy aircraft as she fumbles for her gas mask. Slithers of light from search lights pierce the black abyss and the glow from their beams reveals the silhouette of barrage balloons. Above them from 12,000 feet enemy bombers deliver lethal despatches. Air raids on Liverpool will claim thousands of lives and tonight Gwennie does not want to become part of the grisly statistic.

During the war the Port of Liverpool and Birkenhead docks across the Mersey had become the most important maritime hub on the west coast of Britain. It received around 1000 ships carrying essential food and other materials from the USA and Canada. Inevitably this intense commercial activity can not go unnoticed and following the collapse of mainland Europe the conquered airfields of Norway, Holland, Belgium and France are used to target Merseyside. Gwennie is living in the city and working close to the docks when Liverpool became the second most dangerous place to live in Britain. She is employed by the MoD as a long distance telephone operator. In the early 1940s

Long Distance Telephone Equipment (LDTE) is advanced technology.

In February 1941 a strategic command centre was needed to protect Liverpool's intense shipping activity. The combined operations centre known as the Western Approaches was subsequently established in Derby House, Rumford Street. It monitored an area of the Atlantic Ocean lying immediately to the west of the British isles where the threat of U-Boat attacks urgently needed to be neutralised. The command HQ added a strategic role to Liverpool's existing importance as the west coast's main convoy hub for merchant shipping.

Gwennie was recruited to join a team of LDTE operators working in the newly formed War Rooms. The building contained a 50,000 square foot basement bunker. Operatives were protected from falling bombs by a seven foot thick roof and three foot concrete walls and for this reason was known as the Citadel or Fortress. Today the operations centre has been turned into a war museum authentically preserving the original furnishings and layout. It is highly likely that Gwennie sat in one of the operator's chairs on display in the LDTE switching centre which she would have occupied during her 6pm to 2am night shift. She was quite safe while working. It was the walk to and from the command centre that posed a real threat.

She shared a flat provided by her Uncle Noel in Harlech with her sisters Ellinor and Jane. Due to its close proximity to the docks however the windows were regularly damaged. Since Gwennie's brother, Joseph, was on duty far away in the Indian army, John's Shaw's visits to the city were always welcomed'. He was a practical man adept at all sorts of building repairs. It was however John's desire to protect the three women that stole Gwennie's heart.

There was of course, according to Anthony's older brother, the RAF uniform too.

During the time John was stationed in Singapore Gwennie may well have been living with relatives in Llandudno to be away from her father as it was during this pre-war period that she is believed to have trained at the Hydro Hotel in Llandudno as a Long Distance Telephone Exchange operator. The experience of using telephone switching gear led to her selection at the Liverpool Command Centre. John was captivated by Gwennie and would visit the flat whenever the RAF permitted him leave. There was a Canadian army base located near the flat and he chaperoned her as much as possible. John and Gwennie were from different social classes in a highly class-sensitive era but he was helpful, self-sacrificing and highly intelligent and she was attracted to his daring persona and, unknown to either of them, shared a common experience; they were both the product of dysfunctional families.

Liverpool was protected by a cluster of airfields encircling the city with the fire power of RAF bases in Speke, Cranage and Tern Hill along with other airfields located at nearby Wrexham, Anglesey, Blackpool and High Ercall in Shropshire. Nevertheless their combined military strength could not prevent the Luftwaffe inflicting extensive destruction. Densely populated residential areas housing dockworkers and their families around the Port of Liverpool were inevitably bombed with significant loss of life. Much of the city centre including its main shopping and business areas also suffered heavy bombardment which destroyed some of the city's best-known buildings. Miraculously the monumental and iconic Edwardian baroque Port of Liverpool Building, with its landmark dome, survived eighty air-raids. The deprivations and uncertainties of the Blitz intensified the experience of romance. The first wanted to destroy life and the other create it and the perilous business of surviving carpet bombing underlined the fact that they were living close to death. Each morning came the realisation they had survived to live one more day.

When setting off for the Western Approaches HQ at 6am or returning at 2am in the dark Gwennie experienced the shock of seeing holes where buildings once stood. Records from the period show that entire streets with rows of closely packed family homes of port workers were flattened. How many residents lay amongst the fallen bricks and charred remains? Gwennie and her sisters survived the war although 4,000 Merseyside inhabitants perished and many more were seriously injured. With an uncertain future and the deprivations of rationing and unending danger, the prospect of marriage and love and the mutual concern of two people for one another while living in a dark place must have seemed a dream worth risking. And so it was that in July 1941 John was given a week's matrimonial leave. The couple were married in the Church on the Little Orme, Llandudno and honeymooned in Harlech. There was little point in worrying about the future and on 20 April 1942 Christopher was born nine months to the week in a Nuneaton hospital close to RAF Bramcote where John was serving. This marked the end of Gwennie's Liverpool adventure. Rather than face evacuation to a stranger's house they arranged to stay temporarily in Harlech.

Ellinor, the eldest sister, also left Liverpool after the war. She married George Neves, a Portuguese man, and emigrated to start a new life in Toronto, Canada in April 1948. The couple had one daughter, Jennifer. Christopher treasures a postcard he received from this aunt on their outbound journey showing the SS *Veedam* of the Holland-America Line. The card was addressed to Master Shaw, The Shrubbery's, Thaxtead, Essex. This was one of many RAF postings for John. Gwennie's half-sister Jane also emigrated to Canada and lived in Montreal. Anthony planned to meet her after visiting Daniel Ling who was working at McGill University. Unfortunately while en route Jane died of a brain haemorrhage.

Following the defeat of Nazi Germany John was posted to the Isle of Man to set up a new NATO radar system. His brothers were unable to join any of the Armed Services due to poor eyesight and so Cedric continued to work in Civil Engineering while Geoffrey remained in Rhuddlan where he met his future wife, Rosemarie. At the end of the war he returned to his childhood home of Heacham with his Welsh wife to raise three children.

32

Crazy Cat

Sarah looked through the hatch. Heavy rain etched the surface of rough waves traversing Sydney Harbour. She knew what to expect the moment the shelf cloud approached from the South east. Now was the quiet before the storm. She made coffee, closed her eyes and allowed her thoughts to drift as the aroma filled her senses . . .

She placed the coffee on the tent floor as the sound of a distant avalanche disturbed her thoughts. It was midnight and the other climbers were kitting up for the six-hour climb to the top of Tocllaraja that rises above the Ishinca Valley in the Peruvian Andes. High base camp had been set up at 5,000 metres and the air was noticeably thin. The climb would be demanding and had to be accomplished in six hours if she was to witness sunrise at its most spectacular.

The hope of summiting one of the Cordillera Blanca peaks filled her with the same excitement as when looking up at Sydney's tall commercial buildings and experiencing their intoxicating suggestion of 'opportunity'. It was, after all, these opportunities that paid for her extreme adventures. There had been many near-death experiences such as when collapsing with heat exhaustion ascending Thailand's highest mountain on a bike and then descending its twisting road from Chiang

Mai to Pai accelerating up to 78 kilometres per hour trusting in her maintenance skills and ability to avoid potholes seconds before hitting them.

And here she was in the Peruvian Andes with her first partner James. The Tocllaraja in the Cordillera Blanca range is no place for novices and Sarah was more than ready to be tested. She had summited others all requiring acclimatisation and many days trekking to reach high base camp but the Andes with their unique 70 degree powdery-snow slopes present their own technical challenges.

Elite climbers consider the Nevado Tocllaraja to be one of the easier 6,000 metres peaks to climb. Nevertheless it demands endurance and ingenuity. Nowhere else, even in the Himalayas does soft packed snow cling so tenaciously to inclines as steep as these or give such a convincing appearance of solid platforms as thick snow overhangs high ridges to form cornices that can too readily collapse under foot. These were the deadliest of traps along with glacial seracs whose unstable character wait to fool the unwary. Sarah and James knew the dangers and always hired an experienced guide. The name Tocllaraju, from the ancient Quechua language and spoken by over eleven million South American Indians living in the Andean Highlands, means 'snow-covered trap'. Glimmering in the sunlight, the trap with its various ambuscades rose majestically above the Ishinca Valley, waiting to embrace their arrival. As an experienced climber she knew what was to come. Her hands would become numb with cold and then physical tiredness would give way to mental resilience otherwise known in the family as Lawton stubbornness. She had it in bucket loads as Anthony knew only too well.

Together with James they would scale steep flutings of

powdery snow uncertain of what lay beneath and rappel down rock faces, their lives secured only by a flimsy belay. The one feature that might unsettle her were rickety ladders used by previous climbers to cross impassable crevasses. Seeing these antiques stretched across deep fissures might trigger a temporary paroxysm of anxiety – but at least the guide would test them first. The Andes is characterised by avalanches and lying awake in her tent the sound of ice and rock crashing down a nearby glacier was an intimidating experience.

The view from the porthole had darkened as thick cloud covered the city. The latest spell of intense 12-hour day accountancy had finished and together with her second partner, also James, she would sail to Brisbane to prepare the catamaran for an ocean voyage. It would not be her first. A thirteen-day passage from the Caribbean to San Lucas, Mexico via the Panama Canal to deliver a sixty-five foot yacht had been the most gruelling. It promised to fulfil Sarah's passion for sailing but not as she had expected since with two hundred and ninety five nautical miles to go the wind died. Lack of wind and engine failure combined to severely hinder their progress. Travelling at three knots would threaten their provisions. The cyclone to come and a night of crashing through high waves would be the least of their worries. The adventure would become one of tedious progress and disciplined rationing once the storm had passed.

The journey to Sydney Harbour began twenty-five years ago when Sarah set out in a tiny Optimist Dinghy. Anthony had purchased it for his daughters when they were four and five years old. Here on an off shoot of Burghfield Lake the infants learned to sail and later compete at a safe distance from the adults where

Anthony and his crew fiercely contested their ranking in the Enterprise fleet. It was the open water and backing winds on this disused quarry beside the M4 Motorway that spawned Sarah's love of the sport. One day the adult would race fifty-five foot yachts. The small agile crew member would prove adept at fast spinnaker changes when racing where speed and dexterity are necessary to prevent the sail dropping into the water. This could be a disaster. Spinnaker changes can be perilous and sometimes Sarah was submerged when caught in a Chinese gybe.

She sipped her coffee and reflected on her journey to Australia. She recalled how her parents' divorce had little immediate impact on her or her younger sister's daily routine. Life carried on as normal in so many ways. The parents had managed the divorce thoughtfully to protect them from the deeper emotional wounds of separation and neither Kirsty nor Sarah felt they were a split family. She remembered the summer holidays in the North Devon surf town of Woolacombe Bay. It reminded her how good things can emerge from sadness in life. She had inherited her father's appetite for adventure which had surely been nurtured by the freedoms he allowed. They would be let loose at dawn and take surf boards to the beach and only return when hungry. The space gave them a different kind of responsibility and learning. Rowena would have had a meltdown.

Sarah displayed all of Anthony's stubbornness and it was inevitable that these two strong-willed spirits would clash. Following one such seaside showdown Anthony sent Sarah home on a train. He was heartbroken but Sarah refused to apologise and he would not back down having issued an ultimatum. It was a matter of principle. Life is not a piece of cake, more a messy trifle but happiness can grow out of sadness and mutual respect can evolve out of conflict and the freedoms and conflicts between two strong willed people had given Sarah the fortitude to explore the world. No regrets. Anything is possible she thought as a potentially fatal adventure in the Bolivian Andes came to mind. Without a role model the journey to the summit might have defeated her.

Summiting the 6,088 metres Huayna Potosi should have been well within her capabilities. After a long trek from the village of Tuni she and James reached base camp at an altitude of 4650 metres. Following a satisfying supper they crawled into their sleeping bags at 7pm and prepared for a long cold night until at 10pm they awoke feeling ill. It was food poisoning. Sarah recalled seeing raw meat hanging in the sun at the entrance of the Guide's tent. For the next ten hours they vomited into the snow enduring high temperatures and freezing winds while slowly dehydrating with their water supply spent. Now a climb that should have been easy enough could become foolhardy. What were their options? They could return to Tuni but the long trek in their condition would be uncomfortable and they would be alone. Alternatively they could continue in the hope that after a day or so the illness would pass and their strength return? She remembered her father's teacher Daniel Ling visiting their home when she was a small child. If Anthony had the tenacity Daniel had given him self-belief. Sarah was nine years old but she instinctively felt a deep respect for Daniel. He was a father figure to the family and she knew Grandma Gennie loved him. The whole family held him in high esteem because he'd enabled Anthony to overcome. What would Anthony do in these circumstances?

The wind was howling now and they had travelled far to reach

Huayna Potosi. They decided to continue hoping a recovery was possible. It would prove to be the right decision and following a nauseous seven hour walk across a 5,000 metres pass they were able to reach the Refugio were they could rest and be kitted for the summit. They felt their strength returning as they reached high base camp at 5,130 metres the following day. After a few hours' sleep they would be ready to climb to the summit. As they gazed at the snow covered Huayna Potosi the sense of overcoming an illness was only surpassed by the grandeur of the mountain and cluster of white peaks in the distance that form the Cordillera Real. At midnight they would start their final 500 metres climb. They set off by torch light in otherwise clear conditions until around 2.30am cloud started to descend and it was not long before they found themselves shrouded in a white torchlight world and little vision. They traversed a narrow precipice before confronting a 45 degree wall that had to be climbed. At 5,800 metres the climb consisted of a series of ledges and small crevasse crossings with the feared rickety ladders. Sarah was grateful that the whiteout hid the hazards beside them as she anxiously screamed to vertigo-susceptible James to keep into the ledge.

As they left one problem behind another appeared at 6,000 metres when a steep ridge and near vertical drop of a thousand metres emerged out of the fog. The guide went ahead testing a narrow path of ice. From the far end he shouted instructions that they should follow cautiously one foot at a time as the ridge was extremely dangerous. This would require synchronised movements as they were roped together. There was no room for error now and their concentration was pierced periodically by the guide's anxious shouts of 'PELIGROSO! PELIGROSO!'

(danger!, danger!). Only a 60 metres contouring climb along the thin ridge stood between them and the 6,088m summit which they achieved before the sun rose.

The sky was delicately illuminated enabling Sarah to see the surrounding mountains of the Cordillera Real rising above the cloud. The last section had been a trial of nerves but anxiety is good she thought. It focusses the mind and once she reached the top it began to melt away as the endorphins flowed. She and James had overcome food poisoning and physical weakness. James had struggled with vertigo and Sarah with immobilising back pain. Her ascent had only been made possible because James had carried all the kit. A 20kg load including helmets, ice axes, crampons and an array of snow clothing. They had needed every item. From the summit she looked out onto the curvature of the earth – the reward for her determination to complete the painful climb. During the previous three days there were many times she could have turned back. The challenge had become too hard but now as she looked at the valley below she saw the patterns of tortured ice formations and conquered crevasses scattered beneath her feet – marking the line of her progress.

By contrast the journey to Woolacombe Bay was much easier. Anthony's brother David would drive them to the coast where with the Webb family they would live in caravans beside the sea and be lulled to sleep by the sound of crashing waves. Here, for ten glorious days, adults and children were young and free. She thought of the parents 'ying and yang' personalities; Rowena the risk-averse parent who diligently managed their education and Anthony who never seemed to worry. But they knew he was breaking. There were subtle signs of torment but no emotional dramas although Sarah remembered that if he heard the song

'I am sailing' by Rod Stewart he would quietly weep. He thought he was hiding it from them but the girls knew and would try to give emotional support in their own ways.

In June 2020 Sarah and her new partner James sailed the catamaran to Brisbane. They set about refurbishing the boat in dry dock. It was warmer and cheaper than Sydney's busy marine facilities but the clock was ticking. The work was tiring but also satisfying in the warm Queensland winter. Soon temperatures would soar making manual work impossible for much of the day. She anticipated the next ocean voyage. Perhaps she could entice her father along. She had been impressed by Anthony single-handedly repairing a manhole cover in the drive though blind and completely unflustered. 'He'll be pushed to the limit' she chuckled to herself as her mind wandered and imagined what might have been if she'd been Captain of the Jubilee Trust's tall ship *Lord Nelson*;

'Rouse up you lazy land lubbers. Sleepers awake!

'How deep is the channel Mr Lawton?'

'By the mark, eight fathoms Captain.

'Five fathoms?

'No, eight fathoms. Cor, and I thought I was the one who couldn't hear'.

'Cargo vessel two points off the starboard bow coming out of the fog bank Mr Lawton. Secure the yards tackle if you please. Anthony thought this was supposed to be a holiday. 'Cor flippin eck. Who does she think she is, Captain Bligh?'

'All hands on starboard rail! That includes you Mr Lawton.'

Anthony coped amazingly well given his disabilities but he wasn't always on the ball.

He spoke to a crew member before being rudely interrupted.

'No time for the chattering classes here Mr Lawton. 'Close reef the mainsail!'

'Aye, aye Captain'.

'Mr Lawton, help Mr Morton on the mizzen'.

'But you told me to reef the mainsail.'

'No disputes Mr Lawton and when you've done that clean the heads'.

It was just one thing after another. He thought there would be frequent tea breaks but Captain Sarah liked to push her crew.

'All hands, make sail! Brace the yards to starboard Mr Lawton! And put that smartphone away'.

The wind had died down and Sarah swung lazily in the boson's chair as her thoughts wandered into the distant past and considered her unusual role when growing up as a child, trying to take on some of her father's pain as his eyes continued to deteriorate. How does a child do this? Women mature more quickly than men. She remembered the day of the car crash. He came home subdued and explained how he had hit the door of a parked car as it unexpectedly opened. It was unsettling and she knew he would have to stop but the car was so important to him. Mum had tried to be a caregiver but couldn't cope in the end. It's the old story of hearing people marrying deaf partners. She thought about this as she pulled herself along the gunnel to paint a new area of the hull. She was pleased with her proficiency. 'Not bad for an accountant' she thought. As with her father her 'handyman' knowhow was self-taught. She remembered how Anthony had meticulously maintained their Caversham home. There are many types of love language she thought. Many forms of love. She remembered horse manure being delivered to the front garden. There were great mounds of the stuff. Steaming its sweet aroma. Rowena was not impressed. Sarah thought how Kirsty's interest in medicine had come out of concern for her father. She must have feared for the future of a crazy cat alone in old age, unable to hear or see. Children have more vivid imaginations. The girls' futures were shaped in a childhood harness of freedom and discipline and Caversham Park beside Anthony's house was the place to escape when they visited him at weekends to help with cleaning chores just as Christopher and Anthony had once helped Gennie.

It would take a severe jolt many years later, however, to push Sarah into extreme sports. She was twenty five and had been married for only a few months to her first partner James. She was the typical young career-driven woman seen cycling to work in Lycra on busy rush hour roads. Except the road she was cycling down at 25 miles per hour was relatively empty. Everything was fine as she approached a roundabout beside the Microsoft campus in the Thames Valley Business Park. She had intended to continue across and then was flying through the air. When she regained consciousness she was unable to move her legs as paramedics performed emergency procedures.

The accident changed her.

She realised later how close she had come to becoming another road-fatality and struggled six months to recover from two burst compression fractures of the L1 and L2 vertebrae. Kirsty thought she could never walk again.

And then came the moment when she realised that life is short and fragile and she needed to live it. She would live her best life. No compromises. She told the nurse she would climb out of bed to climb mountains and learn Spanish and move to sport-mad Sydney.

Sarah would strengthen her back through a regime of exercises including weight lifting and rowing exercises to compensate for a permanently deformed spine. Until COVID-19 enforced a rest she followed an uncompromising regime of fitness and strength. She would write her own triumph over adversity story. She would be like her crazy-cat father – live life to the max – no complaining.

Top: Christopher
and Anthony, aged 5.
Right: Lawton family
shortly after birth of
David in Caversham.

Daniel Ling, a teacher at the George Palmer School,
gives nine-year-old Carole Butler a hearing test. Mr.
Ling was the instigator of New Town infants class

Daniel Ling with Carole Day and other pupils using latest hearing technology in the ground-breaking PHU at George Palmer School in 1957.

Above: Thomas Jameson.

Right: Gwendoline
(Gwennie) Lawton.

By the KING'S Order the name of
A/Flight Lieutenant J.C.Shaw,
Royal Air Force,

was published in the London Gazette on
1 January, 1945,
as mentioned in a Despatch for distinguished service.
I am charged to record
His Majesty's high appreciation.

Archibald Sinclair

Secretary of State for Air

Top: Citation for Distinguished Service for Flight Lieutenant John Shaw
Above: David in uniform of a Royal Blues Cadet

Top: Lawton family with Christopher's first car.
Above: Anthony's first 'Ent'

June 9, 2000

Blind match

How on earth can you match race blind? Heather Davies has the story from Queen Mary SC, which was witness to the inaugral Anglo-Italian Sight Impaired Match Racing championship.

Queen Mary SC hosted the inaugural Anglo-Italian Match Racing championship for Sight Impaired sailors on 20/21 May 2000 in Sonars with two Italian teams and two British teams.

The format was for each team to sail four races against each of the other teams, with the top two on points sailing for overall first and second place, and the other teams sailing for third and fourth place.

The course consisted of an upwind and a downwind leg only, with three buoys marking the course; emitting a distinct sound, for the sailors to home in on. The start line was marked by two buoys, the port end marker emitting a single sound and the starboard mark a double sound, the windward mark sound being triggered by a 'bow' on the bow of each boat.

The concept is the brainchild of Alessandro Gaoss of the Homerus Project who sail on Lake Garda, to encourage blind or partially sighted people to have the same sailing opportunities as the sighted. The project by the end of 1999 had taught 54 people to sail from all over Italy and survivors purely on donations. This year Homerus is focussing on taking the concept to other countries.

The competitors were graded against the world blind sailing criteria and the two GBR teams were helmed by Toby Davey and Lucy Hodges. Toby, who won a silver medal in the B3 division at last years world championships in Miami, was joined by Vicki Sheen (bronze medal winner in the B1 fleet) and Stephen Rolt in the GBR1 team. Lucy Hodges helmed the GBR2 team with the help of John Long (bronze medal winners in the B2 fleet) and Tomi Lawton.

The Italian teams consisted of Luigi Berlanza, Giovanni Salvador and Filippa Tolaini in ITA 1 and Federico Zanco, Raul Perindon and Giflota Cioradi in ITA 2, all graduates of the Homerus Project. The Italian teams were supported by the Cantine della Valtenesi e della Lugana wine cellar, who have developed the exclusive bottles of 'Bacco di Homerus'. The proceeds from sales are donated to the Homerus Project, and the bottles are printed with an image of the Homerus boats sailing on Lake Garda.

The racing started on Saturday in very light winds, with only one race completed before an enforced early lunch while the wind tried to get it's act together. The afternoon racing took place in slightly

The winning GBR2 team of Lucy Hodges, John Long and Tomi Lawton

Top: Sailing Robin Ready's yacht off the Ionian islands

Left: 'Blind Match'. *Yachts & Yachting*, 9 June 2000 report Anthony's win at the Anglo-Italian blind races.

Top: Anthony and Sarah sampling coffee in South America.
Above: Anthony at the wheel in the Ionian Sea

Top: Anthony sharing women's bunks; *Middle: Lord Nelson* plaque; *Below: Lord Nelson* awaiting departure from Kochi Southern India.

Top: Nigel Pool learning to guide Anthony; *Bottom right:* Hesta. Faithful and trustworthy companion and guide dog.

33

Adjustments

You need good balance to surf and it is easier to practice on land before taking to the waves. Technique begins with knowing where to lie on the board with feet protruding ready to paddle. The surfer then needs to judge the distance of the approaching wave and to paddle hard with the tip of the board slightly raised to catch it. The difficult bit is raising the chest in order to push up and bring one leg forward with both feet planted squarely on the centre of the board. You must then stand and crouch with one arm pointing to the desired direction. Once this technique is mastered it is possible to turn the board to travel parallel to the rolling wave. It is a wonderful moment when board and surfer become a consubstantial entity.

Did Anthony's daughters surf the world's biggest waves? They could perhaps have found bigger ones but this was not important. What mattered was the experience and knowledge that since they could ride these north Devon rollers anything bigger would just be a matter of practice. They would need a lot of practice during the roller coaster years of their young lives.

The parents separated during their primary school years. Divorced followed. It is a painful memory that will remain with Anthony every time he recalls the evenings when he would read bedtime stories. Then the stories stopped. Anthony moved out to live temporarily with his mother in her nearby home. He remembered his own agony at the age of ten when his father left the family home. The pain at least motivated him to work with Rowena to minimise the fallout and ensure their daughters continuing happiness. The children's lives were now divided between these two homes and Gwennie proved to be a comforting grandmother who helped soften the change. During this early transition Gwennie epitomised the Lawton side of the family which they recalled as warm and welcoming and through her kindness helped influence their choice of careers.

Rowena became concerned for her daughters as she considered the potential consequences of marrying someone with a genetic condition even though she knew their chances of developing RP or Usher 2 were extremely remote. When Sarah appeared to develop hearing problems at a young age Rowena became deeply distressed even though ear infections are quite normal in young children. Anthony by comparison was more free spirited, allowing them to choose their own bedroom décor and displayed a relaxed attitude towards table manners. Then came the body boarding and surfing on annual holidays in Devon with their close friends the Webb family. The Webbs may have thought them feral as they ran wild and carefree during those early seaside trips. If the girls were forced to grow up faster after the divorce they were buoyed by the presence of Gwennie. The girls and their grandmother enjoyed a close relationship and they helped her in the latter stages of her life and discovered that caring for someone who loved them was a deeply fulfilling activity.

Anthony purchased a house in Caversham Park Village five years before marrying his second wife, Chrissie. It was a carefully considered location within the neighbourhood of the family home. He could see blindness approaching and pro-actively hunted for a base that would facilitate independent living. There was a nearby bus stop that gave him direct access to Reading town centre. The house was near shops and opposite a park accessible by a pedestrian crossing. This would give him the opportunity to exercise more freely when he started to use a cane and later with a guide dog. The location would provide everything he would need when his sight finally failed.

During the intermarriage years Rowena would drive the girls for alternative weekend stays with Anthony and would collect them on Sunday afternoon. When the time came to leave there was the depressing sense that he was being left behind in a dark and lonely place. He never used the lighting. At this time the daughters understood his desperation for companionship and an intimate relationship with someone his age although they had little idea of the adjustments this might demand if he suc-ceeded. But they observed the decline in their father's ability to live a normal life as disability progressively restricted his free-dom. When they were visiting they knew they would need to be his eyes keeping clear of his movements and picking things up that he dropped unawares.

There came a time when they felt sailing was too danger-ous but they also recognised that Anthony had always lived with danger and had always taken risks. His tolerance seemed to them to be much higher than that of other people and they regarded it as a gift to him – but it was also unsafe to be with him in the car and they were always on the lookout for approaching vehicles – especially cyclists. Eventually he hit one. Fortunately there were no injuries but Anthony knew he would have to sur-render his licence. His daughters survived the rough and tumble of those years knowing that safety awareness had never been on the agenda.

What risks did Anthony take at junctions as cars speed towards him? He would anxiously turn his periscope to and fro frantically judging approaching cars through his narrow spy-glass vision. He would move into what appeared a clear road only to discover a vehicle appearing as if from nowhere and he would need to break in the mainstream of oncoming traffic before completing the turn. Shadows and bright light were always a problem. Driving into the sun would disturb his vision as would driving under bridges or through tunnels. With hindsight the girls were impressed with his ability to survive on wheels. As Anthony juggled his responsibilities he relied on his nuclear-physicist ex-wife to monitor their homework knowing that her dutiful mind would ensure they completed every task. He knew too that their inherited high intelligence would enable them to surf through the highs and lows of these relentless academic challenges.

When Chrissie came into the sphere of the family it introduced a completely different dynamic. She was the converse of their father yet in one sense they were like minded. She never complained about her disability and like Anthony displayed a rugged can-do persona. But two tough self-reliant people do not make comfortable partners. Despite the frictions Anthony's daughters were aware of the trials Chrissie had suffered surviving a difficult childhood and now struggling with the consequences of poorly managed diabetes in her youth. The girls ultimately recognised she was simply trying to do her best with the life she had been given. They were aware that her strong Christian faith was the source of her strength although they fell outside the centre of her vision.

Anthony sits in an armchair and reflects on the deeply painful adjustments everyone is going through. There is time to relax for a minute or two while it is quiet. Time passes by. From the chair he sees an unmade road of sorts slowly coming down the hillside to the sea. Then it hits him; the realisation that the pain he suffered when his parents divorced had revisited his young daughters. Divorce is an intergenerational curse. He looks up from his chair. Partway down, the road turns beside a cleft and it is possible for him to look up and see the point where the road began its descent. He could see it cascading from the skyline and would have been dazzled if at that moment the sun had passed over the ridge on its diurnal journey to the west. Lower down the valley another route appears out of nowhere. It is little more than a glorified track strewn with stones. It seems to gurgle out of rough-hewn land that is the natural home of gorse and scrub and brambly thicket whose thorns tear at unprotected skin. This rustic track winds its way haphazardly across the slope to meet the larger road, which itself is little more than a wide track, and the two conjoined roads continue as one rounding the curve of the hill. From the top of the cleft it is impossible to see where the rustic road would take a traveller or how far it meanders before joining the coastal highway. The combined road moves across the landscape to carry occasional working vehicles between agricultural buildings. Anyone travelling here would need to be careful. Nevertheless the road is functional and honest connecting isolated hillside buildings and rudimentary habitations. He joined the road knowing that wherever it went he would accept its consubstantiality.

34

Coast to Coast

Anthony knows that if they hit a rock at this speed he and his pilot will be flung from the tandem. But this is not the time nor the place to worry about consequences. The sound of squelching mud and spitting stones is discernible as the cyclists follow a sharp descent through the Kielder Forest on the Scottish boarder. Anthony senses the forest's huge proportions and beauty. Two cyclists; the seeing pilot and blind stoker trusting in each other's ability to synchronise their movements as the tandem hurtles down the twisting forest track. It is an exhilarating experience for Anthony as he melts into invisible surroundings.

'The adventure began in my imagination. I was thinking of new ways to exercise and I thought of cycling and I realised a tandem would enable me to take it up again. As the rear cyclist (stoker) the ability to see is not important. I went to view a used one with a friend and although the stoker end was slightly small I purchased it on the spot. Tandem cycling came naturally as I have a good sense of balance and intuitively know when to lean into a turn. I then found two or three friendly pilots and was so encouraged I joined a group of people cycling in Windsor Great Park.

When Mike, one of my pilots, suggested cycling a coast-to-coast route with a support cyclist John, I didn't hesitate for a moment. We chose the lesser travelled west-to-east route from the Irish Sea at Whitehaven in Cumbria to the North Sea at Tyne-mouth, Northumbria. This includes a large part of the Reivers Cycle Route. Unfortunately choosing to travel from east to west meant we would encounter harsher uphill climbs with shorter spells of downhill ecstasy. At the end of the journey there would be little comfort in knowing the prevailing wind gave us some assistance. The Reivers Route is a 170-mile hybrid on-and-off road trail that meanders through the remote interior of Cumbria and Northumberland and venturing briefly into Scotland'.

The journey presented various problems that began with a puncture when still in Cumbria. It did not augur an easy passage. John and Mike made the repair while Anthony rested sagely against a drystone wall. Unseen in the distance, Skiddaw, England's sixth largest mountain, rose defiantly against a blue sky. 'I contented myself that, with my senses alive, I could experience more vividly what my eyes could not see; a moment in paradise. I knew we were high up in an open landscape although I could only imagine the beauty of what stood before me. I remembered an earlier cycle in Derbyshire as we travelled along a converted railway cutting, passing under an unusually tall road bridge and when moving from an open vista into woodlands. The reflections of sound informing changes in my surroundings. Reflected sounds help me 'see' things differently. I am not in the dark. My imagination is alive. I see in a similar way to a bat using echolocation which helps me to navigate obstacles. The bat makes a sound in its throat and the amount of time it takes for the sound to return to its ears enables it to mentally construct a picture of its surroundings. I don't make sounds but simply rely on naturally reflected noise. Bats and blind people see differently to sighted people. The phrase 'blind as a bat' is a complete misnomer. Bats can see almost as well as humans although I can't see as well as a bat.

I remember reaching the Scottish border at Carlisle but do not enjoy cycling on busy A-roads where lorries rush past as shadows and I feel their fleeting and unwelcome proximity. Every night sleeping in the soft bed of an inn is bliss. It is now that I realise my error. Not only am I in pain and needing a hip operation but the stoker frame that seemed adequately sized when I purchased the tandem is now clearly too small for such an arduous journey. Even when I set the saddle to its maximum height my knees keep hitting the handlebars forcing me to sit as far back as possible to allow room for my legs to move. This crouched position became extremely uncomfortable and even during the early stages my body was screaming to stop at the end of the day. I knew this ride would take me to my threshold but this was one of the reasons for doing it. The other was to escape the nagging ache of bereavement that still clung to me four years after Chrissie's death. The ache was part of every dreaded ascent and welcomed descent. If the climb became too much for me we would walk rather than stand on the peddles when cycling. There were three people on the tandem. I am sure Chrissie enjoyed the challenge.

Mike had been one of Chrissie's friends. When she died he cycled from Land's End to John O' Groats to raise money for the Oxford clinic that had nursed her. This 170 mile coast-to-coast tandem journey would therefore be a minor challenge by comparison but it was an endurance test for me. We had planned a six month preparation period but circumstances kept Mike in his home town of Tring and we managed only a few practice cycle rides together during that time. Ultimately we accepted that our preparation would be a matter of training-on-the-job. The secret to enjoyable tandem cycling is not to fight the pilot and Mike would not have been aware of me as I became his shadow mimicking his movements. At the outset we established certain procedures so that I would know in advance what was about to happen.

Mike had known Chrissie in her twenties as they both lived in Tring and were part of a group who loved outdoor adventure. Chrissie was a risk taker even then. The group would squeeze into an old van full of camping equipment and head off to north Wales driving along dangerous mountainside roads in all weathers. Youth gave them a different perspective of risk and four wheels provided the access to adventure in Tryfan and Glyderau, Snowdonia. Mike recalled how Chrissie always chose challenging routes requiring sure-footed concentration but these isolated terrains could become fearsome places if cloud descended at an inconvenient time. She undertook these physical challenges suffering diabetes. She was young and wanted to overcome the limitations imposed by disability and medication. It is a testament to her resilience that she climbed these mountains. She was an indomitable spirit. The coast-to-coast journey did not heal my bereavement but the preparation period softened it. The months spent thinking about the coast-to-coast challenge provided a welcome distraction.

Sometimes the off-road trails in the borderlands become little more than steeply inclined dirt tracks that extract lung punishing work for every yard yielded. We cross lonely, moaning, windswept terrain with the melancholy Cheviot Hills to the north before descending into the Kielder Forest and Kielder Water. A comfort break is planned at a teashop in Bellingham but by now I am exhausted and my inflamed hip so painful I feel I cannot continue. Such is my distress I am prepared to spend the night sleeping in the open rather than climb on the bike again. When the owner of the teashop sees my condition she becomes concerned and phones a nearby pub. They have spare rooms but it is at the top of another hill. The thought of a bath, hot meal and long sleep in a soft bed give me the resolve to make the ascent and I promise myself I will write a letter of appreciation to the owner. I have no doubt the pub will be superior to anything the bracken covered floor of Kielder Forest can offer – especially as Lynx are about to be introduced to this wild area. My enthusiasm on the penultimate day evaporates quickly as I am in some discomfort. Sailing kept me fit but it was a different type of fitness to that required for long distance cycling and I was mistaken to think I could manage. A hired van was waiting for us in Newcastle and just as I was thinking of asking John to collect it rather than finishing the journey the road turns into a long descent. We bank into corners in unison as we gather speed. The coast-to-coast cycle ride had taken me out of my comfort zone but now I feel elated.

Despite the hardships there were few arguments during the long ride. This may have been helped by my daily discipline of accepting the frustrations of blind life. When I make a mistake with home repairs or suffer breakages and spills in the kitchen I accept these mishaps philosophically. There is no one there to help me and giving in to angry outbursts would only impoverish my mental health. As a consequence I have never had an accident with equipment. I begin by imagining what I am trying to do and become calm, careful and concentrated. Perhaps this is a form of meditation. When I start a project I know I shall lose things. I will lose my way and have to start again. This is part of the game, part of the challenge but I never become impatient with myself; slowness is a necessary discipline.

One of my last major projects before lockdown was to build a garden shed to hold a larger tandem. This required some planning beforehand. I am passionate about what I do and I will need to remember where to find every tool in the future shed. The blind are capable of achieving far more than sighted people imagine. This is one of the topics of my talks to various groups. I explain that blind people do not have visual references but as someone who lost his sight in later life I do have visual memories and it is important to remember personal history. The past is powerful.

During lockdown I was asked to do zoom presentations but I refused because I knew I would struggle. I prefer face to face meetings which are more tactile. Reflected sounds in a room tell me so much about the audience and my surroundings. A computer screen could never deliver this palpable information which enables me to interact with the audience to raise the quality of the event. Lockdown is phenomenally hard on blind people, especially those who are going blind. Eighty percent of information comes through the eyes so it is not surprising why the threat of sight loss is so distressing. Touching people is an important way for blind people to relate. This is how we see them. But any contact is forbidden by Covid. Hugging is important but for two years I am not allowed to hug anyone. This simple human signal of friendship was taken from me and I did find it challenging. Although all outdoor activities are cancelled

I can at least play chess and walk Hesta. Everything else stops. Tandem cycling in Windsor Great Park, rambling with others, competing with the bowls team, practicing archery, attending Reading Football Club, sailing at Burghfield or joining a friend on his yacht in Greece – all cancelled. I live alone and it would be easy to succumb to this extreme isolation but I also know that when the blind demonstrate how they can cope sighted people are encouraged. I survive Covid by playing chess online and maintaining my house and garden. Everyone needs to navigate through times of darkness. This is why I want to share my experiences. I came through the darkness of Chrissie's death.

We are five miles from Newcastle when two spokes snap in the rear wheel. A week of cycling over rough terrain has bought them to the end of their endurance. Spokes are the most modest, underrated, and understated components. As the wheels rotate these thin rigid wires support the weight of bodies and luggage and absorb the impact of unforgiving terrain. They are stretched and compressed over and over again. We force acceleration though these wiry pillars every time we pressed on the pedals and transmit the stopping force every time we applied the brakes. They were pummelled and punished throughout the coast-to-coast ride.

We stop to replace them and it provides another welcome break for me before crossing the iconic bridge into Newcastle. I feel elation as we emerge out of the urban areas towards the coast. This was Tynemouth and I could smell the sea. We drive the final miles to Whitely Bay. This is the end. A satisfying sense of relief follows but for people like me the end just leads to new beginnings and the end of the pain now rekindles a desire for future adventure. I decide I shall have to do something wild once a year and my justification will be charity work. Sky diving, car racing, zip wire walking – wing walking.

The three of us gaze at the sea and say nothing.

35

A Dog to Guide Me By

It was many years ago. Anthony was at home harnessing his guide dog for the first time without the help of a Guide Dogs' Association trainer. Formal training is over but there is still much to practice as the duo of dog and master learn to trust each other. Trusting his life to a dog does not come easily. There are many hazards; crossings without audible safety alerts, silent electric cars, distraction's from passers-by and confusion about commands.

Anthony's house is conveniently located near parkland across a busy road. It provides the perfect short journey for practice and exercise as they seek to become a competent team. It is also a place of happy memoires. This is the place Chrissie spent many hours with her pet dog and after her death it became the natural place to scatter her ashes. Anthony arranged to have a memorial park bench installed. There is an inscription that was Chrissie's motto, 'Always look on the bright side of life'. The bench provides a landmark place that he heads for when walking. He purchased the house after his divorce because of its location to amenities knowing that he would need easy access to these services in his blind future. As he recalls, 'I knew it would be relatively easy to find my way away round the neighbourhood. There is a bus stop nearby with a regular service to the centre of Reading. The purchase paid off handsomely'.

His home is a place of tranquillity. The interior décor is stylish, the rooms are furnished and the whole house is utterly tidy. When visitors step through the door they are greeted by a Victorian grandfather clock which originally stood in the Harlech home – a true heirloom. There is not a thing out of place – a necessary discipline for someone who has no sight as Anthony explains: 'I memorise the place of everything in the house. Every detail is logged in my mind. I know if surfaces are clean or dirty by touch but I need weekly visits by a cleaner to tell me if there are any stains and to confirm the house is presentable. I am able to select shoes and clothes by touching them. Fabrics have unique and subtle textures. The problem of matching socks is solved by buying only one colour. My favourite colour remains red which was first confirmed in my 1956 St Thomas' end-of-year School report and this preference has never changed. You may wonder how I select clothes from the wardrobe and I solved this problem using my smartphone. I simply use an app to video the clothes and a family member or friend then tells me what I am looking at. I also use it if I need help identifying dates on food packaging or if I lose something and people can help me find the item.

It is important to me to know that the house is not only presentable but a touch stylish for receiving visitors. I satisfied this need by appointing an interior design company. There was no point using brochures so I discussed décor with their designer and by feeling the fabrics to help with colour coordination. I see the emerging design in my imagination and the final design is bought together with feedback from two or three friends – usually women'.

Anthony manages his home in the same way he manages his participation in a chess tournament where he sees the pieces in his mind and remembers each move. Only one household item is occasionally out of place. This happens every morning when Anthony gets out of bed and Hesta (his guide dog) runs around with his slippers before dropping them by his feet. Strict discipline ensures food safety. Anthony has rarely inflicted food poisoning on himself or others. Food is kept in different shaped containers; square, round and long and he always buys the same brand-shaped packaging. If there are any duplicated shapes he uses elastic brands to identify the contents of tinned food. He also uses a device called Penfriend which is an electronic labelling system from RNID. He knows how to apply the bands because he is given help in supermarkets when selecting food from the shelves. Two rubber bands for beans three bands for peas and so on.

Contrary to expectations Anthony does not run a basic kitchen. 'I love cooking because of the sensations of touch, smell and taste and I enjoy combining flavours and entertaining friends. When it comes to food preparation I am extremely practical and devise best practice to ensure I work methodically with proven routines. This is helpful when I want to experiment with recipes. Finding the right ingredients is rarely a problem. My ability to create interesting dishes safely is helped by a lifetime's insistence on high standards whether in the workplace, DIY, car repairs, sport, or in the kitchen'.

When away from the tranquillity of his home Anthony expertly helps Hesta guide him around the hectic streets of Reading town centre. After five years of working together Hesta gives him confidence and constant companionship – they are a united team and when she is working on busy streets he must ensure no one distracts her. Anthony's high-performance hearing aids help him discern street noises whether they come to him directly or are reflected.

Sounds of buses are different to cars. He can judge their speed and proximity. He can hear the bustle of people around him. There is a strict routine. He holds the harness handle and the lead in his left hand but uses the right hand for commands. Hesta provides safety but she cannot guide Anthony if she does not know the route and he needs to work out these things sometimes with the help of friends or by asking pedestrians the way. There is a strict reward scheme and he feeds Hesta a small treat whenever she has successfully navigated an important part of the route. She is attracted to cafés and Anthony has to be mindful that he always has control of his guide whenever the smell of food fills the air. The dog's harness, like his cane, is red and white to indicate dual sensory loss. When boarding buses Anthony commands Hesta to find an available seat. Hesta is now a deeply experienced guide dog and copes well in the most frenetic environments accompanying Anthony wherever he goes.

Working together requires total concentration by both dog and handler and day dreaming when out and about would be a disaster. It takes around two years to train a guide dog and their average working life is about eight years – such are the demands the work places on the animal. As many as forty five percent of puppies do not reach the standard required. The most reliable breed has proven to be a cross breed between Golden Retriever and Labrador and Anthony is fully aware of his responsibility as an owner.

'My priority is a happy dog and I ensure Hesta has a lot of play time. It is a bit like encouraging a child. Fun time is a responsibility because it maintains the mental health of a dog that costs £65,000 to train. The Guide Dog Association has to raise around £45 million a year to meet demand.* I need to maintain discipline and standards at all times because a guide dog can be ruined in the first year of work and cannot be retrained. We both make mistakes and so the relationship is one of constant learning and correction – improving communication and dog management. Hesta and I have been working together for eight years and will need to retire soon and this will be a wrench because Hesta and I have a wonderful working relationship. She is an exceptional companion. It will be tough for me to start again from the beginning with a new guide. I am passionate about guide dogs and want to share my passion with audiences whenever I am invited to give a presentation in town halls, schools, care homes and company lunch time meetings and wherever people want to know how a guide dog and owner work together'.

* Figures 2019

36

Listen

'I became a listening volunteer for a charity that supports people with degenerative and progressive sight loss. I thought my experience might encourage others. I wondered how the older Anthony Lawton might have helped the younger man on the telephone should he ever call me.

'Hello Anthony it's your Younger Self'

'Hi Younger Self, how are you?'

'Oh, OK apart from few bruises'.

'How did you get the bruises?'

'I tripped over a bag someone had left on the pavement'

'Oh nasty. Were you using a cane?'

'No'.

'Why not?'

'I told you before. I don't want the stigma of people thinking I'm blind'.

'But you are going blind and you will need to be able to use a cane when most of your sight has gone'.

'I don't want to think about that now.'

'Why'

'I'm frightened at the thought of being blind.'

'I remember being frightened. But you need to prepare now while you still have some sight'.

Waving a cane in front of you on a busy pavement can feel awkward and embarrassing especially when you still have some useful sight but someone setting out on the journey to blindness must learn to use it effectively. The common reason the partially sighted refuse to use a cane is pride. They don't want people to know they have sight issues. I thought the same way until I narrowly escaped a serious accident and that really focussed my mind I can tell you. All my life I tried to hide behind a façade of self-reliance. I don't need your help thank you very much. But it can be a lonely place and I don't want other people to make this mistake. I wish I hadn't made it. I would ask my younger self probing questions to gently nudge him in the right direction.

'What will you be doing in five years' time?

'I don't know'

'You ought to be thinking about that now'.

'Yes I suppose so'.

'What are you doing to prepare for the time you are totally blind?'

'I read that scientists are working on a cure. I'll be alright.'

I speak directly, 'You are living in a dream. You are going to lose your sight Anthony. You need to be preparing for that eventuality.'

I can say this because I am talking to myself.

Sometimes people don't want to hear the truth. They would rather hide in comfortable delusions and false hope. So I repeat the same questions. Many people in the early stages of blindness go into denial. They are afraid to face up to the reality of a future without sight.

Sometimes it takes an alarming experience to shock them into taking action.

'Are you getting out enough? Are you meeting up with others who are blind? You need to'.

'Do you get out enough Anthony?'

'Yes' I say defiantly.

'Tell me one interesting thing you did recently since you are now deaf and blind'.

'I went wing-walking for charity'.

'What's wing walking?'

'They strap you to a chair on the top wing of a biplane above the pilot. And then the pilot does loop-the-loops'.

'Isn't that very frightening?'

'Not if you take a sedative first'.

It concerns me that my younger self isn't yet ready to face up the challenges that will sometimes feel overwhelming. There isn't a lot of help out there for the blind so it is important to know what is available locally. The best way is to join a group. Learn from others. It is important to build some resilience. I would ask my younger self if he getting any equipment? What equipment does he have? He told me he went out and lost his way recently and I voice concern but he says he managed to find his way back eventually. I think how difficult and distressing that must have been especially without a cane. No wonder he tripped over a bag. I think life becomes easier when people who are going blind are able to face the truth and think about how they will manage. The world becomes less threatening and fear loses its immobilising grip. What might I say to my younger self if I had the opportunity? If it was just one thing it would have to be an encouragement.

'Don't worry Anthony. I can tell you it will be all right'.

Alas, I cannot help my younger self but as a listening volunteer for a charity that supports people going blind my experiences and mistakes can help others starting out on the same road. I am pleased that although I was born deaf with the aid of technology I can listen. Sometimes that is all anyone needs'.

37

Whaam!

Anthony is sitting on a sofa. His grandchildren are playing around his feet and he hears their voices full of excitement. It is 2016. He thinks how young and vulnerable they sound and finds himself fearful for them. Life is fragile and uncertain. Then he has a kind of epiphany as he sees his mother sitting beside him bearing the same pain and fear when she is told that her four year old has to leave home to attend a boarding school for the deaf and dumb. He has thought about this before. Then it was a shallow appreciation of what she might have felt but now it goes deeper. For a moment he is experiencing her despair as her son's wellbeing is taken out of her hands. Nobody listens.

It is as if he sees a painting except he is not looking, he is in it. Suddenly he is the fighter pilot in Lichtenstein's Whaam! He experiences the coruscating blaze of the rockets against the vibrant blue sky. He is his mother in 1950. For the briefest moment Anthony looks and knows exactly what is being lived. It is only a moment and then the intensity of the emotion and the immediacy of the image evaporates into a watery memory.

It lived for a moment; the intensity and actualisation of memory. The bright primary colours of red and yellow and vibrant blue. Now he is the onlooker outside the action knowing there was a moment when he felt the heat of the flames and saw the brilliance of the colours burning into his eyes. The image of his mother a life time ago burning with intensity. He understands the consequences of family history, what motivated her and shaped her fears. The two were joined for a moment in a shared experience; mother and son.

AUTHOR'S NOTE

Silent Pigeons Coo is a memoir and family saga that explores Anthony Lawton's struggle to live a normal life and the subterfuge required to achieve this goal having been born with a 70 decibel hearing loss and discovering encroaching blindness in his teenage years. The struggle portrayed in Silent Pigeons Coo is a true story as is the portrayal of the interweaving complexities of family history. It explores the consequences of choices made by previous generations and their impact on succeeding ones and briefly searches genealogy in search of two distant relatives who unwittingly donated two faulty genes that jump generations to bequeath Ushers syndrome type 2. The storyline is punctuated with researched historical episodes and a sprinkling of fiction to describe incidents and conversations swallowed up in time. The main thread of the story is about finding a fulfilling life despite genetic disadvantage but it also explores setbacks that affect most people whether due to self-sufficiency, divorce, bereavement or the complications of nursing secrets. The memoir reveals the troubling metamorphosis of a young person seeking to transfer allegiance from family to peer group at the time of a growing dualistic debate between sign and oral communication. The search for acceptance will lead to a crisis of language and identity. The outcome will define his adult life. Today most deaf children and young people follow an oral approach with some using a sign support system[1]. At 76 Anthony continues his passion for extreme adventures with the justification of serving the needs of charities. These include Guide Dogs for the Blind, Retina UK and RYA Sailability. During four years of interviews I have sought to reveal something of the struggle. Dr Daniel Ling OC, Anthony's Teacher of the Deaf said: *'people who overcome a problem can have an abundance many people are deprived of. In fact more so because they have overcome . . .'*

Usher syndrome type 2 is an inherited condition that affects both hearing and vision. The severity of hearing loss varies from mild to profound and is known as sensorineural because it affects the ability of the cochlear to convert sound energy into nerve signals which the brain learns to separate as intelligible noise such as language. Sight loss is caused by degradation of the retina and known as retinitis pigmentosa (RP). *Silent Pigeons Coo* will speak of retinitis pigmentosa or RP during Anthony Lawton's childhood and Usher syndrome type 2 in his later life.

ABOUT THE AUTHOR

John Moore's writing career began as a London advertising copy-writer and later as a freelancer working for large communication groups such as Charles Barker and Ogilvy & Mather. His previous books were paid commissions. *Transforming a Treasure* was written for Exchequer Partnership and describes the £197m transformation of Government Offices Great George Street (1 Horse Guards Parade). *Celebration of Innovation. A History of Autotype 1868–2005* records more than a century of achievements prior to the company being acquired by a US organisation. It is dedicated to Kitsy Mitchell a former Autotype chemist who provided the historical research.

Postscript

As a boy and adult I have been told I do not listen. I do listen but not at the appropriate moment. I am aloof. You could argue I suffer from learning difficulties. I would argue that I simply have an undisciplined mind. But I did listen to Anthony for over four years as he struggled to recall distant emotions and colour-faded events. There were moments when chapters in the developmental stages of his story reduced him to tears as painful memories resurfaced. Learning is often painful and life is about dealing with disappointment. Anthony mostly succeeded rather than succumbed and bought joy to people's lives. This is the gift that comes out of his disability. The term neither stigmatises nor insults him.

His story appealed to my imagination because the little boy made a promise to himself as did I and he remained true to himself. Even at the age of four, despite the external evidence and the bullying voice of the world, he promised he would escape the legacy of a deaf and dumb school and compete in the bruising hearing world. His defective hearing would always be an impediment but he would rise majestically above it just as the mountains of his birthplace dramatically rise from the sea. Technology would make this possible. This and the long hours of striving with his mother and Daniel Ling. They would provide a rich inheritance when the light in his eyes faded into darkness.

Was the search for distant married cousins a wild goose chase? In such a tangled web of family relationships that are not consistently listed in the records it is possible that cousins married somewhere along the inter-generational line. But they would need to carry the rare gene condition. Usher type 2 syndrome and retinitis pigmentosa are related inherited diseases. The consultant ophthalmologist at the John Radcliffe Eye Hospital in Oxford asked the question in the interests of medical science and Anthony and I tried to explore the possibilities. Does it matter? It matters to science but to Anthony? His attitude would be 'just get on with it'. He is participating in a blind chess competition in Windermere today. He expects to win.

John Moore

P.S. It has been a joy and sometimes a challenge rediscovering the past with Anthony – especially the distant emotional landscapes. But travelling without the inner man would have been to explore a barren landscape. His struggle has been a gargantuan one but so was that of his father and mother. We have all persevered.

Chapter References

Chapter 1. Silent Pigeons Coo

1. Birmingham Mail. (Updated 30.05.2010-24.10.12) https://www.birminghammail.co.uk/news/local-news/former-resident-of-haseley-hall-in-warwickshire-247862

Chapter 4. Story of the Deaf

1. 100 Years of Deaf Education and Audiology at The University of Manchester. Dr Laura Dawes. https://documents.manchester.ac.uk/display.aspx?DocID=23262

Chapter 5. Four-Year Void

1. https://www.facebook.com/

Chapter 6. Sunrise Reading

1. *The Royal Berkshire Hospital. 1839–1989* by Margaret Railton and Marshall Barr.
2. Obituary – Remembering Dr. Kevin Patrick Murphy by Roger Willis. Published by the British Society of Audiology: https://www.thebsa.org.uk/obituary-remembering-dr-kevin-patrick-murphy/
3. *So many hearts make a school: The Centenary of the George Palmer Schools, Reading* by Daphne Barnes-Phillips and James Barnes-Phillips
4. Deaf Children. Report published in the 1960 Country Borough of Reading Report 'Education in Reading 1955-1960' Ref: R/GB

Chapter 7. Dr Daniel Ling OC

1. The power of hearing: the story of Dr Daniel Ling' Elaine & Eli Tal-El. Funded by the Canadian Film Board in 2000.

Chapter 11. I Chose My Identity

1. *Juhani Pallasmaa Eyes of Skin: Architecture and the Senses*. Wiley & Sons Ltd 2005
2. United Nations Declaration on the Rights of Persons Belonging to National or Ethnic, Religious and Linguistic Minorities, adopted by the General Assembly

Chapter 15. The Horse
1. *The Times* 26 August 2017.
2. *How do profoundly Deaf Children Learn to read.* Susan Goldin-Meadow and Rachel I. Mayberry. Learning Disabilities Research & practice. The Division for Learning Disabilities of the Council for Exceptional Children

Chapter 20. Surviving Chrissie
1. https://jst.org.uk/life-on-board/

Chapter 21. Black Sea. Bright Sky
1. https://timesofindia.indiatimes.com/india/Indian-waters-third-worst-for-pirate-attacks/articleshow/27761370.cms?prtpage=1

Chapter 24. Implosion
1. https://historicengland.org.uk/listing/the-list/list-entry/1321948

Chapter 26. Heron, Enterprise and Challenger
1. http://ryasailability.tv/videos/clubs/small-changes-big-difference/

Chapter 28. Lawtons' Liverpool
1. See family tree apprentices

Chapter 31. The Shaw War
1. No18 (P)OTU

Appendices

Appendix A

Statistics relating to education of deaf children.
- There are at least 45,060 deaf* children in England – a reported decrease of 3% since 2019.
- 78% of school-aged deaf children attend mainstream schools. 6% attend mainstream schools with resource provisions, 2% attend special schools for deaf children whilst 14% attend special schools not specifically for deaf children. 1% are home educated.
- 23% of deaf children are recorded as having an additional special educational need.
- 14% of deaf children use an additional spoken language other than English in the home.
- 88% of deaf children communicate using spoken English as their main language in school or other education settings, 7% mainly use spoken English together with signed support whilst 2% mainly use British Sign Language.

Extract from Consortium for Research into Deaf Education (CRIDE) 2021 England report on its annual surveys of local authority specialist educational services for deaf children.

* The term 'deaf' refers to all degrees of deafness. Of the profoundly deaf people about a third use English exclusively, one third combine English with British Sign Language (BSL) and one third use mainly BSL as their primary source of communication. BATOD uses the terms 'deafness' and 'deaf' and not 'hearing loss' or 'hearing impairment' in its publications as these are not usually welcomed by deaf people (Paul Simpson). In *Silent Pigeons Coo* the term 'hearing loss' is used within memoir sections that come from a mid-century society that was in transition in terms of understanding the deaf community: such a society would not have recognised users of sign language as a linguistic minority. Anthony was a child of this era.

** Paul Simpson. co-National Executive Officers for BATOD (British Association of Teachers of the Deaf after a career as Housemaster at Mary Hare School, a peripatetic teacher in Leicestershire and Oxfordshire, a lecturer at the University of Birmingham training Teachers of the Deaf, the head of the sensory support team in West Sussex, head teacher of Mill Hall School for deaf children, a teacher in a resource base in Buckinghamshire, an author of educational guidelines for the RNID and a governor of two schools for the deaf. He is also the Vice-President of FEAPDA (the European Federation of Associations of Teachers of the Deaf; Fédération Européenne des Associations de Professeurs de Déficients Auditifs) having been President for 13 years. Paul trained as a Teacher of the Deaf from 1984–1986.

**Schools for the Deaf now tend to have a different clientele as many accept children with additional disabilities and take a different approach using Makaton or other sign support approaches. Newborn hearing screening, access to hearing aids and cochlear implants and improved understanding of language development mean that most children can use sound to acquire oral language through listening.

***Edward Moore. Retired Teacher of the Deaf (ToD), MA Special Educational Needs, Former President of BATOD, Trustee of the Ewing Foundation & of the Ovingdean Hall Foundation.

Appendix B

Legacy of the Ewings.

Paediatric audiology at The Royal Berkshire Hospital has benefited in so many ways from the pioneering work undertaken at the then named Victoria University of Manchester Department for the Education of the Deaf established in 1919 and now renamed Centre for Audiology, Education of the Deaf and Speech Pathology. It was a prototype for teaching deaf people to listen and speak. It was here that paediatric audiology and teaching the deaf became two interconnected spheres of expertise pioneered by Sir Alexander Ewing and Lady Irene Ewing. They laid the foundations in terms of knowledge and practice. Lady Ewing's career was influenced by her own loss of hearing due to otosclerosis, a bone growth disorder in the middle ear.

The university's engagement in deaf education and audiology was originally made possible by a generous endowment from James Jones, a Victorian businessman in the Manchester cotton industry when his orally educated deaf son, Ellis Llwd Jones, died of disease while serving in France during the First World War. The son had been taught in a private school for the deaf in Kent run by the leading advocate for oralism of that time, Susanna Hull. The schools expertise benefited from the involvement of Alexander Graham Bell who used 'visible speech', a method based on phonetic spelling developed by his father Professor Alexander Melville Bell. Bell's family were widely associated with elocution and speech as his mother and wife were both deaf. This interest in the deaf also contributed to Bell's future inventions of the telephone and rudimentary hearing aid technology. There was therefore a strong thread of knowledge and practice in oralism bequeathed to Ellis which he used to support his involvement in deaf welfare in near-by Rochdale. After his premature death Ellis' father believed the best use of his son's estate would be most appropriately used to fund the first university-based training programme for teachers of the deaf. This might not have been the case if an identical initiative at the time had not temporarily foundered in London.

The first head of faculty was Irene Rosetta Goldsack who was developing new child-centred methods of oral teaching at the Henry Worral School for Deaf Infants. Her progressive methods however were distrusted by the old guard. She believed speech acquisition needed to be embedded in activities that interested the children rather than follow accepted methods of repeated pronunciation drills. She thought mere learning of words a futile activity and wanted them to speak spontaneously through their involvement in activity. Thus speech and language would develop as part of the child's broader development. Irene Goldsack was therefore already evolving methods of teaching at the Henry Worral School that she would further develop with her future husband and collaborator, Alexander Ewing.

A breakthrough moment occurred in 1928 when Alexander Ewing's screening investigations provided scientific proof that children who were regarded as totally deaf had in fact residual hearing. This discovery had previously been made known by Dr James Love at the Glasgow Institute for the Deaf who at the turn of the century reported that 90% of his pupils were known to have residual hearing. The Ewings went on to demonstrate that when this tiny amount of hearing was 'harvested' using technology the ability to hear became the most important motivational factor in promoting speech and language learning. At this time the use of hearing technology alarmed many deaf schools because they believed technology would hamper a child's ability to lean to lip read. Nevertheless the discovery helped strengthen the Ewings three core beliefs. These were the importance of early intervention, early parental engagement and the parent's continuing role in speech practice.

Two or more decades later Anthony would be a beneficiary of this single-minded approach to oral deaf education. It was important to Gwennie that Anthony learnt to speak and was subsequently mentored by Irene Ewing. She supported her son fastidiously when he was taught by Dr Daniel Ling, a Ewings protégé who was appointed by West Berkshire Education Authority to spearhead an experiment that would transform the teaching of the deaf in Reading.

The Ewings 'child-centred' clinical approach led to hearing tests that were developed as games. The Tunnel Test enabled a child to respond to sounds that altered in pitch providing the information for an audiologist to reveal the child's 'auditory sensation area' – the audiogram. The Distraction Test was devised in 1944 and was so successful it was used into the 21st century. These tests relied on a behavioural response from the child such as turning the head when a sound was heard. Some years later the Royal Berkshire hospital would lead the way in the use of these clinical methods and pioneer new ways of testing new-born hearing by measuring physiological responses.

The behavioural approach allowed the Ewings to study hearing patterns in normally-hearing new-borns. This may seem unsophisticated now but was a breakthrough moment in the 1940s. The Ewing's tactile approach and games were applied to early childhood screening programmes for seven to nine month-old children and was used by health visitors as late as 2006 although results could vary according to the tester's skills.

In 1933 when Thomas Littler, a physicist, joined the Ewings team he contributed a vital advantage. One of his most notable achievements to British audiology was his work for the Medical Research Council in designing a hearing aid to be issued by the future NHS. Littler responded with the MEDRESCO. It was not an arbitrary development but combined expertise in the medical, surgical, education and electro-acoustic technology although manufacturing capability of the day limited its practicality. The device produced reasonable but not good sounds and even some adults found the weight cumbersome because of the heavy batteries. Nevertheless by bringing together science, technology and education the multidisciplinary work in Manchester enabled deaf children in Britain to engage in the hearing world. The work led to the Ewing Foundation in 1952. Its aim was to provide opportunities for a wider range of deaf children. It also arranged for group hearing aids and speech-training units to be demonstrated to teachers and parents in schools across the country. Alexander Ewing was knighted in 1958 for services to audiology and deaf education. Both he and Lady Irene Ewing and the Manchester department had created a template for the advancement of clinical practise, technology and teaching practices in schools1.

1. 100 Years of Deaf Education and Audiology at The University of Manchester. Dr Laura Dawes. https://documents.manchester.ac.uk/display.aspx?DocID=23262

Appendix C

Describing the daily routines of crewing a tall ship across the Indian Ocean to Australia risked introducing a note of tedium to Chapter 22 for anyone not attracted to the idea of such a long and potentially hazardous adventure. These were therefore selectively described. If however the idea of crewing a tall ship across a major ocean sparks your imagination the log of Robin Ready, Anthony's JST buddy for the second leg from Singapore to Freemantle, provides detailed insights from routine duties to more spectacular experiences.

The Log of Robin Ready
J.S.T. Sailing Singapore to Fremantle. 6 June – 22nd July 2013.

Day 1 – Thursday June
- Up at 5.30am. Heathrow: 9.40am flight
  Day 2 – Friday 7 June
- Arrive at Singapore 9.30am (their time)
- Problems with customs due to not accepting my papers of boarding the *Lord Nelson*, after several telephone calls got it sorted
- Train to the harbour approximately 45 minutes (very hot 30 degrees)
- Entrance to the quay was through a shopping centre
- Arrive on board at 1.30pm, sign up for the *Lord Nelson*
- Met up with Tony (my buddy) visual impaired allocated bunk 26
- 4.00pm had training briefing along with the rest of the crew
- 6.00pm had a meal, view the cable cars across the harbour along with the tower blocks and the setting sun, showered and turn in at 8.30pm
Day 3 – Saturday 8 June

- 2.00 – 4.00am had Harbour watch with Tony
- 9.00 – 10.00 had happy hour followed by training – ropes handling and up and over the yard arms
- Walked along the water front and explored the area
- 6.00pm meal – showered chatted and turning at 9.00pm
- 4.00pm had training briefing along with the rest of the crew

Day 4 – Sunday 9 June

- 4.30am took on board all our supplies for the voyage
- Free morning also another up and over the yard arms
- Had lunch then took Tony shopping to obtain a keyboard for use with his mobile phone
- Walk along the seafront and looked around the Sentosa Leisure Park
- Mess duties at 5.00pm – turn in at 10.00pm

Day 5 – Monday 10 June

- Up at 7.00am for mess duties finished at 3.00pm
- Left harbour at 9.00am accompanied by a Local band then out into the South China Sea
- 8.00pm–12 midnight for watch duties

Day 6 – Tuesday 11 June

- Up at 7.30am for breakfast – Sailing along the north coast of Sumartra
- Had rope and chart training during the day
- Double rainbows around the Sun and clouds – very beautiful
- Meal – shower – turn in at 8.00pm
- 12.30pm – 4pm watch

Day 7 – Wednesday 12 June

- 12midnight – 4.00am watch
- Over the equator at 3.54am into the southern ocean
- Sail tying training
- 1.03pm took part in the initiation of crossing the line
- 4.00pm – 6.00pm watch
- Evening meal – turn in at 8.00pm

Day 8 – Thursday 13 June

- 4.00am – 8.00am watch
- In the Java sea with the Borneo coast on port side
- 6.00pm – 8.00pm watch
- Meal – shower – turn in at 10.00pm

Day 9 – Friday 14 June

- 8.00am – 12.30pm watch
- Had a talk on the weather patterns
- Still in the Java sea
- 8.00pm – 12.00 midnight watch

Day 10 – Saturday 15 June Up at 7.30am – breakfast
- Assisted in giving a talk with Tony and Craig on visual impaired persons (both visual and hearing impediment), it was well received by other crew members
- 12.30pm – 4.00pm watch – (very hot)

Day 11 – Sunday 16 June
- 12 midnight – 4.00am watch – still in the Java sea
- Reported weather conditions to Greenwich main records centre
- Breakfast – then church service
- Sail training – saw flying fish and dolphins
- 4.00pm – 6.00pm watch
- Meal – shower – turn in at 10.00pm

Day 12 – Monday 17 June
- 4.00am – 8.00am watch
- Sail handling – more flying fish and dolphins
- 5.00pm – 7.00pm – mess duties
- Meal – shower – turn in at 9.00pm

Day 13 – Tuesday 18 June
- 7.00am – 3.00pm – mess duties
- Entered Bali harbour at 9.45am – waited for customs and harbour pilot
- Berth at 1.30pm at the southern end of the island
- Had a local walk around dinner on board – turn in at 10.00pm

Day 14 – Wednesday 19 June
- Up at 7.00am – breakfast, no Duties
- 9.30am – 4.30pm – toured the island
- Visited temples and paddy fields in the World Heritage site
- Royal Dinghy Sailing Club arranged a dinner on board also a group of orphanage children giving a Hawaiian dance on the quay side

Day 15 – Thursday 20 June
- 2.00am – 4.00am Harbour watch
- Up at 7.00am – Breakfast
- Left the quay at 9.30am out through the harbour by 11.00am
- Sails up and sailing with all sails

- 4.00pm – 6.00pm duties
- Dinner – shower- turn in at 9.00am

Day 16 – Friday 21 June
- 4.00am – 8.00am duties
- Breakfast – sails up – very lumpy and rolling seas
- All sails down at 6.00pm
- 6.00 – 8.00pm duties
- Saw a large shoal of Flying Fish

Day 17 – Saturday 22 June
- Up at 7.00am breakfast
- 8.00 – 12.30pm duties
- Wind eased – motor sail
- Flying fish and Dolphins
- Fishermen exchange a number of barracuda fish for a bottle of whisky and 9 dollars – all parties happy with the deal
- Had the fresh fish for the evening meal
- 8.00 – 12.00 midnight duties

Day 18 – Sunday 23 June
- Up at 7.00am breakfast
- Sails set – church service
- 12.30 – 4.00pm duties – report weather conditions to Greenwich
- Not visiting Christmas Island, due to very heavy swells and a very bad forecast
- Dinner at 6.00pm

Day 19 – Monday 24 June
- 12.00 – 4.00pm duties
- Set sails – then course on Celestial navigation
- Duties 4 –6.00pm
- Dinner and turn in at 9.30pm

Day 20 – Tuesday 25 June
- 4.00pm – 8.00pm duties
- Egg drop – we came 2nd
- Very choppy seas and deep swells
- All persons with disabilities not allowed up on deck
- Mess duties 5.00 – 7.00pm
- Dinner and turn in at 9.30pm

Day 21 – Wednesday 26 June

- Mess duties 7.00am – 3.00pm duties
- All persons with disabilities not allowed up on deck
- Sails Up – very choppy seas
- Dinner and turn in at 9.30pm

Day 22 – Thursday 27 June
- Up at 7.00am – breakfast – sailing but very lumpy seas
- All persons with disabilities not allowed up on deck
- Duties 12.30 – 4.00pm
- Talk on Navigation and Celestial positioning
- Dinner and turn in at 8.30pm

Day 23 – Friday 28 June
- 12.00am – 4.00am duties
- 20 knots of wind very rough and pitching and rolling
- 4.00 – 6.00pm duties
- Talk on what ropes do and which operates the sails
- Dinner and turn in at 8.30pm – (very weary)

Day 24 – Saturday 29 June
- 4.00am – 8.00am duties
- Sight of Cosus Island at 7.05am
- Moored in the bay within Cosus island at 9.30am
- Australian customs come on board taking 2 hours to check the every one and every thing on board
- Emerald seas and baby sharks 5 foot long, also the seas breaking on the reefs
- 6.00pm drinks given out then watch the 'SODS' video made by the ships crew – (I want to be Free by Queen)

Day 25 – Sunday 30 June
- 7.00am breakfast on deck (no duties as a free day)
- Dinghy to the island (choppy seas very wet)
- Walked around the island then had a swim
- Dinghy back to the ship and saw a few dolphins
- Shower – Bar-B-Q on board – turn in at 9.30pm

Day 26 – Monday 1 July
- 7.00am breakfast on deck
- 9.30am up anchor and sail away from the island – all sails up
- 12.30 – 4.00pm duties- good swell and 20 knots of wind
- Shower – turn in at 9.30pm

Day 27 – Tuesday 2 July
- 12.00 – 4,00am duties
- Sailing 20/25 knots of wind – big swells
- Engine alarms 1.30 am – one engine fails to start and operate
- 4.00 – 6.00pm duties
- Still sailing – just the wrong course south west

Day 28 – Wednesday 3 July
- 4.00 – 8.am duties
- 30 knots of wind speed
- Both engines now working
- 6.00 – 8.00pm mess duties

Day 29 – Thursday 4 July
- Mess duties 7.00 – 3.00pm
- 35/40 knots of wind – motor sail
- All persons with disabilities not allowed up on deck
- Travel 1578 miles

Day 30 – Friday 5 July
- 12.30 – 4.00pm duties
- All persons with disabilities not allowed up on deck
- 35/40 knots of wind – big swells

Day 31 – Saturday 6 July
- 12.00 – 4.00am duties
- All persons with disabilities not allowed up on deck
- Big swells 4/ 5 metres – 40 knots of wind heavy rain showers
- 4.00 – 6.00pm duties

Day 32 – Sunday 7 July
- 4.00 – 8.00am duties
- All persons with disabilities not allowed up on deck
- 35/40 knots of wind – big swells and heavy rain
- Motors off – sails up – wind easing
- 6.00 – 8.00pm duties
- Still heading south

Day 33 – Monday 8 July
- 8.00 – 12.30pm duties
- All sail up winds 10/15 knots – sea slight
- Tidying up of the film show
- Catching up on sleep

- Turn in at 8.00pm
- 8.00 – 12.00 midnight

Day 34 – Tuesday 9 July

- 12.30 – 4.00pm duties
- Change of course – 100 degrees (eastwards)
- All sails down – on motors – sunny and very light winds
- 5.00 – 7.00pm mess duties

Day 35 – Wednesday 10 July

- 12.00 – 400am duties
- Beautiful Galaxy of Stars
- Motor sail – flying jib and main sail 105 degrees
- Cloudy and sunny with very light winds

Day 36 – Thursday 11 July

- Mess duties 6, 45 – 3.00pm
- Motor sail – light winds 850 miles to Perth
- 6.00 – 8.00pm duties

Day 37 – Friday 12 July

- 8.00 – 12.30pm duties
- All sails set – winds from the north 15/30 knots
- 8.00 – 12.00 midnight duties

Day 38 – Saturday 13th July

- 12.30 – 4,00pm duties
- Very heavy rain all morning – very big swells
- Talk on French canals trips by Allan

Day 39 – Sunday 14 July

- 12.00 – 4.00am duties
- Great array of stars
- North winds 15/20 knots – light swell – very heavy rain all afternoon
- Church service
- Hartigutrau talk by John
- Engine room tour
- 4.00 – 6.00pm duties
- 4050 miles covered

Day 40 – Monday 15 July

- 4.00 – 8.00am duties
- Change of tack at 5.00am all sails adjusted
- 6.00 – 8.00pm duties

Day 41 – Tuesday 16 July
- 8.00 – 12.30pm duties
- All persons with disabilities not allowed up on deck
- Storm force 10 – 50 knots of wind
- Very high seas waves with 6 meters troughs – rain and showers
- All sails up
- Boat speed 14.2 knots (highest ever recorded for the *Lord Nelson*
- 8.00 – 12.00pm duties
- Storm force – wind speed recorded at 60 knots -very heavy swells
- Boat Speed recorded 12.6 knots
- Knock off the helm by heavy shower and very large swell
- Very difficult to helm due to the swells and the listing of the ship
- Completely exhausted after watch

Day 42 – Wednesday 17 July
- 12.30 – 4.00pm duties
- Calmer seas – 20 knots of wind
- 5.00 – 7.00pm mess duties
- 6.00pm – sighting of Rotnest Island
- Moored up at Fremantle at 9.30pm
- Voyage of 4,578 nautical miles

Day 43 – Thursday 18 July
- 7.00 – 3.00pm mess duties
- Afternoon free
- Walk around Fremantle
- Had a meal out with Tony – it was great – (real ale and steak)

Day 44 – Friday 19 July
- 6.00 – 8.00am harbour watch
- 8.30am breakfast
- 11.30am – signing off from the ship
- Afternoon free walked around Fremantle with Tony
- Booked mini bus to airport

Day 45 – Saturday 20 July
- Free day
- Two coach trips around Fremantle – visited the indoor market
- Walked along the coast and explored Fremantle fort
- 10.30pm – pick the mini bus to the airport
- Stayed over night

Day 46 – Sunday 21 July
– 9.00am – flight to Singapore airport
– Waited around 4 hours – look around the butterflies garden
– Flight to New Deli airport
Day 47 – Monday 22 July
– Waited 14 hours
– Flight to Heathrow – arrived 6.30pm
– Coach delay left at 9.30pm
– Arrive Pool valley at 10.05pm
– Train to Shoreham – by – Sea
– Arrived home at 23.55pm
– Again completely exhausted after 47 days

Appendix D

Family History of the ancestors of Anthony Lawton
Comment on commissioned research by Daniel and Rachel Masters

Daniel and Rachel Masters were commissioned to undertake limited re-search into the ancestry of Anthony Lawton. The principle objective was to identify distant cousins who married and had offspring since an eminent physician at the John Radcliffe Eye Hospital had asked this question. Inherited diseases such as Usher 2 require two faulty genes to cascade through the generations to bestow this unwanted heirloom.

Identifying historic cousins now shrouded in mostly forgotten personal history is not as simple as it might seem. Records are not always complete or infallible and open to interpretation. This research was limited to accessible records on the internet and via local resources (largely Ancestry and history websites, and newspaper archives). Thus, some records and leads have not been fully followed up, leaving room for further research.

Subsidiary work was also done to uncover any evidence of historic illness in the family and again the sources provide no evidence of illness connecting the generations. The Masters also searched for broader family interconnectedness and added an appendix to the report that includes an outline of the family history, including some further points of interest and a family tree and profiles. The family tree is illustrated in this Postscript section.

The Main Report concludes that due to the limited scope of the research the cousins' hypothesis remains an unproven hypothesis. The report goes on to examine the interrelatedness of the family and shows there is only limited evidence to suggest that any interrelations between two cousins took place in Anthony's direct line.

The paternal three-time great-grandfather of Anthony, William Starmer, married a Mary Checkley. It is possible that William Starmer's paternal grandmother was also a Checkley; if true, this could mean William and Mary were related, however, further evidence would be required to confirm this conclusion. Similarly, Anthony's maternal three-times great-grandmothers (Mary Davies and Anne Owen) both had the maiden name 'Jones'; yet again, further research would be required to confirm any relations. Some surnames reoccur, for example, Davies is a prominent surname on the maternal side, and a later member of the family married a Davies: Anne Jane Jameson (Gwendoline Jameson's sister) married an Evan Ffrydlas Davies – though the evidence suggests that this is not a relation. Likewise, in census data some family surnames have appeared on the same street as other parts of the family: for example, both the surnames Davies and Parry appear in the family tree, and in census data for the Davies line, the surname Parry often occurs in the same street; however, again, no evidence links them to the Parry family in this family tree. Importantly, this evidence should be treated carefully as these surnames, especially those that are Welsh, were very common. Therefore, whilst there is evidence to suggest cousins could have married each other, the evidence is not strong enough to draw any conclusions without further research. The report continues:

Eric Jameson's (Gwendoline Shaw's, nee Lawton, Great uncle) marriage to Flora Reed (John Shaw's aunt) may explain the link which led to the marriage between Gwendoline Lawton and John Shaw. This research has also shown a strong North Welsh and Northern England link on the maternal side. On both sides, Gwendoline Lawton had links with North Wales: Llandudno her maternal side (through the Davies), which may explain Gwendoline Lawton's return there to get married to John Shaw (indeed family marriages had taken place at the Davies owned St George's Hotel), and Anglesey and Denbighshire on her paternal side. There were also links with Liverpool, through the direct Lawton line, and Yorkshire through the direct

Jameson line – both providing a possible explanation for how the family ended up in Liverpool. Also, on the paternal side research has shown strong links to Northamptonshire and to London. Through Arthur John Shaw (Anthony's grandfather) the family can be traced far back in Northamptonshire through both his mother and his father's sides. While through Evelyn Alice Reed (Anthony's grandmother) there is evidence that the family has strong links to London. The evidence here is circumstantial, but suggests that the family had strong geographical interconnectivity, and explains the links with different geographical regions.

No evidence has been found to suggest a history of illness in the family. William Starmer Shaw was noted in the 1911 census as being 'feeble minded'. However, he was sixty-one in 1911, and in previous census records, going back to 1851, no such illness was recorded for him; thus, it is most likely that this was a product of old age. Even so, William's symptoms do not suggest anything similar to Anthony's condition. Otherwise, no other evidence of issues in the family history have been found.

Other points of interest

The Maternal Side: Gwendoline Mary Lawton

The Lawton Line: includes Thomas, Cooper, Poyser, Kendrick, Parry

This side of the family begins with Thomas Owen Alfred Lawton (b. 1884). His family was a mixture of Liverpool, North Wales and Anglesey. Following the death of his wife, Gwendoline Lawton (nee Jameson), it has been suggested that he married again, though the name of his second wife has 'remained a mystery'. No marriage certificate has been found to confirm his second wife, however, according to the 1939 census he lived with a Maber J. Lawton (b. 1899) and both were married. It is unclear if they were married to each other, and if they were, whether this was a second or third marriage. On Thomas's father's side there is a long succession of Thomas Lawtons going back to at least 1818 when Thomas's great grandfather, who would become a 'joiner and fixer', was born. The next Thomas Lawton (Thomas's grandfather), began as a 'farmer's apprentice' before also becoming a joiner. It was Thomas's Grandfather's brother (Joseph Alfred Lawton) who set up the coach building company in 1870. The nephew (William Lawton Goodman) who expanded the business was the son of Joseph's sister (Thomas's Great Aunt) Margaret Lawton. The next Thomas Lawton (Thomas's father) would first begin working as a 'coach maker' between 1871-81. Joseph's probate lists a Thomas Lawton as 'Carriage builder's manager', but the 1911 census has Thomas Lawton listed as a 'worker' at the business. Thomas Owen Alfred Lawton's first recorded occupation (1901) was also as a 'coach maker', but this changed to 'motor engineer' in the 1911 census, and similarly an 'engineer' in the 1939 census – possibly corroborating the business ventures into to motor cars and planes. Otherwise, Thomas's other direct ancestors were predominantly farmers, though his maternal grandfather, Owen Thomas, became a 'leather dealer' in his later life. Thomas O. A Lawton did have an Aunt called Ellinor Lawton, who had married a Lewis M V[incent] Evans, though no link to Harlech was found.

The Jameson Line: includes Davies, Owen, Jones, Mounc[s]ey, H[K]ey, Smith and Wade

This begins with Gwendoline Jameson (b. 1883 – née Davies), who died around the same time as giving birth to her third child Gwendoline M Lawton (nee Jameson) in 1920. Her family is a mixture of Yorkshire and North Wales. Her oldest known direct ancestors were farmers, except her maternal great-grandfather William Owen, who owned an Inn, the King's Head, in Llandudno. This inn would be inherited by Isaiah Davies who had married William Owen's daughter (Anne Jane Owen). Sources (see footnote to this paragraph) suggest Isaiah Davies was innovative, having managed to gain permission to build the St George's Hotel which would be the first of several famous hotels built in the region. Sources also suggest that illustrious guests have stayed at the Hotel, including Napoleon III, Bismarck and several Prime Ministers. It also has Grade II listed status. After Isaiah Davies, the hotel would continue to be run by his wife, before being inherited by their son, Thomas Pugh Davies. On the paternal half of Gwendoline Jameson's family, William Jameson (her grandfather) would also move from being a farming family, to owning an Inn, and it has already been suggested that his family would set up a photography business, though this research has found no evidence of this. Her father, Thomas Jameson, would spend much of his early life living with his Uncle George and Margaret on a '50 acre' farm in Ellesmere, where he is recorded as a 'farm servant'; between 1871 and 1881 he became a secretary at the Liverpool YMCA and this was registered as his occupation until his retirement and death.

The Paternal Side: John Chadwick Shaw

The Shaw Line: includes Starmer, Burnham, Checkley, Chadwick and Parlett.

The Shaw line is from Northamptonshire. Arthur John Shaw, Anthony's grandfather, had been an Organ Builder and Tuner and so was Anthony's father William Starmer Shaw, who may have started the Organ Building and Tuners company 'W. S. Shaw and Son. Ltd'. The company doesn't exist now but was still in operation up until at least the late 1970s. In a copy of the Northampton and District Organist Association newsletters a tuner's visiting card from W. S. Shaw and Son Ltd., dated 1975, can be found. It is possible that both Arthur and William trained in this profession in Islington, London, because they both spent time there; Arthur was there in 1901 as a student and William married there in 1873, when he may have also been studying. William Starmer Shaw was a shoe manufacturer before he became an Organ Builder, which seemed to have been a family business, as after his father died his mother and his older siblings, were all recorded in the censuses as boot and shoe manufactures, and his father, Benjamin Shaw, and his maternal grandfather, William Starmer, had been shoe makers. William Starmer Shaw's wife, Elizabeth Chadwick, was from London; however, her mother's side of the family, the Marshalls, appear to have come from Northamptonshire too. On her father's side of the family, the Chadwick's and the Parlett's, came from London and Hamptonshire. Her father, Mentor Augustus Chadwick, was a merchant until his 40s and then became a public accountant in his late 40s/early 50s. His parents died young, and he spent most of his childhood in an orphanage, therefore there isn't much information on them, but Mentor's sister's marriage records that their father had been a solicitor. The orphanage where he and his sister grew up was called the London Orphan Asylum and was set up by a Rev. Andrew Reed in 1813 (no evidence has been found to prove that this Andrew Reed is related to the Reed line but that side of the family was from London, so it could be a possibility). The orphanage emphasised that children from respectable circumstances would have the first claim to the charity.

The Reed Line: includes MacDonald, Sadd, Bealer, and Mann.

The Reed line is from London and Scotland. The Scottish line begins with Mary Christina MacDonald, the great grandmother of Anthony Shaw, whose father was recorded as John MacDonald on her marriage record. Mary married a William George Charles Reed, a civil service clerk, whose family was from London. His father, William Henry Reed , was a school master, which meant that the family moved a lot and therefore William G. C. Reed wasn't born in London like his parents and grandparents before him, but in Buckinghamshire. William H. Reed was married to a Susannah Caroline Sadd and, including William George Charles Reed, they had three children. In the 1891 and the 1901 census Susannah wasn't living with William H. Reed but was still recorded as married, where as he was living with a Lydia Reed who was recorded as his wife and in the 1901 census he and Lydia had a son called William Alfred Phillip Reed. No records of a divorce between William and Susannah, or a marriage between William and Lydia, have been found, therefore it is possible that he never married Lydia and started a second family. William Henry Reed's father, George Reed, and many of his siblings, were fishmongers and William worked as a fishmonger for a period of his life too. Susannah Caroline Sadd was also from London and her father, John Sadd was a paper stainer (the making of wallpaper) and then from his 40s onwards a house decorator.

Adoption: Sylvia Reed and Wendy Lowe

There is a newspaper article [included in the physical copy] about a Wendy Lowe who had discovered that she had a sister who was given up for adoption and believed her mother, Sylvia Reed, may have also given a son up for adoption. Based on this article, it seems certain that her mother is the same Sylvia Reed (1926-1988) on our tree; she was the daughter of Albert Reed, the great uncle of Anthony Shaw. Wendy Lowe believed her mother stayed with an uncle and aunt, called Geoff (a piano tuner) and Rosemary, while pregnant with her son, possibly between September 1942 and June 1943. However, it may not have been her aunt and uncle that she stayed with but in fact her cousin, Geoffrey Edwin Shaw and his wife Lilian Rosaleen Jones, also known as Rosemarie. The only issue is that Geoffrey and Rosemarie were not married in 1942/3 and did not marry until 1948. It would be of interest to know if Wendy Lowe found out if she had a brother and if so what happened to him.

Printed in Great Britain
by Amazon